Wayne Gretzky:
COUNTDOWN TO IMMORTALITY

Leisure Press
P.O. Box 3
West Point, N.Y. 10996
(914) 446-7110

Wayne Gretzky:
COUNTDOWN TO IMMORTALITY

by Barry Wilner

A publication of Leisure Press
P.O. Box 3, West Point, N.Y. 10996

Library of Congress Catalog Card No. 82-83475

ISBN 0-88011-084-8

Front cover art: Ted Watts
Black and white photographs: Bill McKeown
Color insert photographs: Bruce Bennett

CONTENTS

DEDICATION

I would like to dedicate this book to my family for its patience, understanding and guidance.

ACKNOWLEDGEMENTS

I would like to thank the following people for helping compile this book: Ron Andrews; Joel Blumberg; Dennis D'Agostino; Phil Esposito; Ken Gesner; Rodger Gottlieb; Mike Griffin; Dan Leary; Norman MacLean; Bill McEwen; Jim O'Connell; Fred Pietila; Allyne Price; Terry Price; Gene Quatrara; Ken Rappoport; Mark Stulberger; Pete Wevurski; Helene Wilner; John Ziegler.

Gretzky destroys 50-in-50 record

retzky scores

LANDOVER, Md. (AP) —
National Hockey League's rec
scored two Edmonton goals
other as the Oilers defeated

Gretzky nets his 7[illegible] goa

Gretzky sets points record

EDMONTON, Alberta (AP) — Vayne Gretzky scored three goals nd added two assists Friday night, mashing his own National Hockey League single-season point record and leaving him one hort of the goal-scoring mark as the Edmonton Oilers defeated the Hartord Whalers 7-4.

NHL

Gretzky's second consecutive five oint game gave him 166 for the season, two more than the record he established last season. The th- oals, one in each period, g- 1-year-old scoring wiza- ess than the mark of 7- y Phil Esposit- Bruins.

Gretzk- ach

retzky named NHL player of month

ONTREAL (AP) — Center Gretzky of the Edmonton ed his domination of ey League Player- Tuesday whe for 20 assists he picked up in 11 games. He edged center Bryan Trottier of the New York Islanders for the or. Gretzky and Trottier had game played by their during the

Oilers 9, North Stars 6

EDMONTON (AP) — Wayne etzky, Dave Lumley and Jari rri combined for eight goals — ee each by Gretzky and Lumley — d 16 points to pace the Edmonton ers to a 9-6 win over the Minnesota rth Stars.

Gretzky's goals gave him 38 in 35 mes. He also picked up four assists give him 90 points for the season d keep him in range of his target of 0 points in 40 games.

Gretzky gets 90th goal, 200th point

CALGARY, Alberta (AP) — Wayne Gretzky boosted his amazing National Hockey League scoring totals to 90 goals and 103 assists Thursday night by scoring twice and setting up two other goals as the Edmonton Oilers

NHL

..NHL notes

NEW YORK (AP) — For the time this season, Wayne Gretzk n named the National H gue player of the week gue announced Monday.

he Edmonton Oilers ed four goals and had six hree games — all Edmont es — and notched game-w ls in two of the triumphs.

retzky, who turned 21 Tu ls the NHL with 61 goals ts after 51 games, giving oint lead in the scoring ra is tops in the NHL in ga goals with eight.

ased on his current pace, ld score 96 goals and 21 season.

Gretzky is spotlight tonig

Channel 9, 8 p.m.

LANDOVER, Md. (AP) — The mpbell Conference, led by record-eaking scorer Wayne Gretzky of e Edmonton Oilers, seeks a second raight victory over the Wales Conference in Tuesday night's National ockey League All-Star game.

A crowd of 18,130 is expected to fill e Capital Centre, where only one llout has been attracted during the

first decision last year.

Coach Al Arbour of th Stanley Cup-champion Ne landers directed the Ca their breakthrough. But, u lignment of the conferen be coaching the Wales around.

Adding to the confu Ogrodnick, the Detroit lef scored the Wales' only go and left wing Bill Barber

Gretzky aiming for 100 goals

DENVER (AP) — After extending his record National Hockey League point total to 206 with two assists and a goal in Edmonton's 6-6 comeback tie with Colorado

COUNTDOWN TO IMMORTALITY

Wayne Gretzky, NHL scoring champ of the Edmonton Oilers, is honored with the Seagram's trophy.

Game 1, vs. Rockies at Edmonton Game 2, vs. Canucks at Vancouver Game 3, vs. Kings at Los Angeles

Some would compare Wayne Gretzky's skate to immortality with O.J. Simpson's 2,000-yard season for the Buffalo Bills. Others said it was like winning tennis or golf's grand slams. Or hitting .400, with 65 homers and 200 RBIs in one year.

But Gretzky gave little indication of what he had in store for the sporting public as the 1981-82 season began. In fact, the kid was nearly invisible during the opening week of the season.

Against the Rockies, Edmonton scored a smashing 7-4 triumph, paced by two goals from Jari Kurri, Brett Callighen and Garry Unger. As for Mr. Gretzky, he contributed an assist on Kurri's second goal.

That's it. One measly assist in a seven-goal game. Had The Great Gretzky lost the touch? Did the Oilers need him in light of the balanced attack they displayed against Colorado?

Is a puck black? Is hockey played on ice? Is Wayne Gretzky the most dangerous scoring threat in all of sports?

"It was fun watching the other guys filling the net," said Gretzky, ever the team man.

There was no fun for the Oilers two nights later in Vancouver, where the Canucks battered them 6-2 behind Thomas Gradin's hat trick. Gradin, a smooth center from Sweden who is vastly underpublicized, scored Vancouver's first three goals and blanked Gretzky, who seemed to have trouble eluding the hardworking enemy pivot.

"Gradin showed tonight how good a two-way player he is," said Vancouver coach Harry Neale. "Whenever he had to play Gretzky, he did the job. And he put the puck home when he got the chance."

Riding a virtual schneid, Gretzky took his lone assist into the third game, against the Kings in Los Angeles. Edmonton registered another 7-4 win and Gretzky scored the tie-breaking goal and also picked up an assist.

The Kings would play a fateful role all year for Gretzky and the Oilers. He would victimize them for some of his biggest offensive outputs. And LA would victimize the Oilers when least expected.

For now, however, Gretzky was off to a relatively slow start against three of the league's non-powers.

"But we're 2-1 and that's what's important," he claimed. "If we win two of every three and I only score once in a while, so what?"

Game 4, vs. Jets at Edmonton

The Winnipeg Jets had entered the NHL along with the Oilers, Quebec Nordiques and Hartford Whalers in 1979. Their stay in the NHL had been a difficult one.

"We were raped," Jets general manager John Ferguson succinctly put it in regard to how his club was treated upon joining the NHL from the World Hockey Association, which folded. "They went after our best players and left us some slim pickings in return."

Ferguson steadfastly held onto his draft picks rather than deal them for some short term, limited success. And he went with young, untested talent, suffering now but with high hopes for the future. Last season, the Jets were 9-57-14 and, in one stretch, went a league record 30 games without winning.

This, thought Sather, was the perfect team against which to give first-round draftee Grant Fuhr his initial start in the Oilers' net.

Fuhr had been so impressive in training camp that Edmonton was able to send veteran Ed Mio—who had been their No. 1 goalie for the last two seasons—to Wichita of the Central Hockey League.

Fuhr, the only black goalie in the NHL, is a native of Edmonton who played junior hockey in Victoria. He was considered the only NHL-calibre netminder available in the draft and, even though Sather had a young, potentially spectacular goalie in Andy Moog—one of the main stars in the playoff upset of Montreal the previous spring—and vets in Mio and Ron Low, he grabbed Fuhr as the eighth pick of the opening round.

Moog started and played disappointingly in the first two games, then Low took the nets for Game 3. Now, it was the 19-year-old Fuhr's turn to show what he could do.

He would do so in style but in a losing cause as the Jets—who went on to the biggest improvement by an NHL team in one season, from 32 to 80 points—humbled the Oilers 4-2 before the only non-sellout crowd the Oilers would have in Northlands Coliseum all season. Fuhr made 32 saves, many of them with catlike quickness and unbelievable recoveries.

Sather felt his choice had been justified.

"I think you will see some great things from that youngster," said the coach, who couldn't have known how quickly his prediction would come true; Fuhr would not lose in his next 24 starts. "It's a shame the rest of our players didn't put in the effort he did."

The Jets expressed total satisfaction with their performance, which defenseman Dave Babych termed "probably the best we've had since I've been here." Considering that covered just three games more than one season, it was hardly surprising to hear such an assessment from Babych.

Selected second overall in the 1980 draft, Babych had spent a rough rookie season, learning the ropes on the ice while the Jets were hanging themselves night after night. One of the few things he was able to enjoy as a freshman was watching Gretzky perform.

"Holding him to one goal is a real accomplishment for us," he said after the game. "I think it's a sign of how much better we are that we not only can come in here and beat the Oilers, but we didn't get destroyed by Gretzky.

"There are times when you sit on the bench and you almost want to clap your hands at some of the things he does. One day, I'm going to shake his hand and hope some of the magic rubs off on me."

Get in line, Dave.

Practice makes perfect.

Game 5, vs. Flames at Edmonton

The rivalry between the cities of Calgary and Edmonton is a bitter one. A pair of frontier boom towns in oil-rich Alberta, Calgary and Edmonton are similar in many respects. But the fortunes of their hockey teams could not differ more.

Last season, the Flames won a playoff series for the first time in their history, including their eight years in Atlanta. They not only won a playoff series, they won two before being ousted in the semifinals by Minnesota.

Still, hardly anyone noticed such an achievement, partially because the Flames beat Chicago and Philadelphia while the Oilers were stealing the headlines by upsetting Montreal and pushing the Stanley Cup champion Islanders to six games in the quarterfinals.

And don't think for a minute that the folks in Calgary were happy their team was being overshadowed during its finest hours by one from their provincial competitor.

The Flames' home rink, the Calgary Stampede Corral, seats just 7,234. It's always filled. It's loud. When the Oilers are in town, the noise is near deafening.

Conditions are similar in Edmonton, though the arena is big and modern. There are no empty seats to be had—except, of course, for the previous game against Winnipeg—and, when the Flames come in, the fans spare no one in the red uniforms from their contempt.

Many observers picked Calgary to skate off with the Smythe Division crown this year. Judging by their performance in this game, an 8-4 Oiler rout, the Flames will be lucky to make the playoffs.

"We were pretty rotten," admitted Flames center Kent Nilsson, who scored twice. "We didn't let Gretzky hurt us too much but we didn't stop their other guys either."

Those other guys were Mark Messier, with two goals, and Kurri, who had four assists. Gretzky had a goal and two assists.

"If you look at Calgary as a team we have to pass in the standings, then this is very encouraging," said Sather. "It was good to see us dominate a team like the Flames."

Gretzky was happy with the eight-goal attack after the loss to Winnipeg.

"When your offense stalls like we did against Winnipeg, it's a good sign to bust out with eight goals in the next game."

Game 6, vs. Black Hawks at Chicago

Gretzky's first big night of the season came six games in, when he notched a goal and three assists in a 7-5 loss to the Black Hawks. It was the first of what would become almost a routine achievement for Gretzky, a four-point night.

But, for one of the few times all year, Gretzky's standout performance would be eclipsed by an opponent. Chicago's Darryl Sutter scored three times to pace the Hawks' triumph.

But Gretzky was on the mind of several observers, including Stan Mikita, one of the greatest centers ever to lace on skates. Mikita was a smart player, one who possessed many moves and used all of them to turn opponents inside out. Still, he marveled at Gretzky's skills.

"He dominates the game like Bobby Orr in his prime, Gordie Howe, Bobby Hull, Maurice Richard and Guy Lafleur," said Mikita, whose name could easily be placed in that select company. "I won't venture to compare him to Orr but nobody ever dominated the game at his age the way he has. I only played against him a few times, but it didn't take long for me to find out he's as deceptive as the devil.

"His biggest asset is that he controls the play. He can speed it way up or slow it down—whatever he needs to do to accomplish his objective."

Mikita compared Gretzky to Jean Beliveau, the great Montreal center who was as smooth as freshly laid ice and as dominant as anyone in his heyday.

"But Gretzky does a lot of things no other player has done," added Mikita. "I won't say he's unstoppable but he's awfully close to it right now.

"The best way to play Gretzky is to keep him from getting the puck. That's obvious. But go out there and try to do it and it's something else.

"He can make game plans obsolete."

Gretzky also might make set line combos obsolete. In the loss to Chicago,

CALLIGHEN
18

Sather played his superstar center with nearly every forward on the team. It was a pattern the Oilers coach would continue all season, a maneuver which would reap a bountiful harvest of goals and points for virtually all of Wayne's linemates.

"I've used him on several line combinations," said Sather. "Tonight might have been the most I've shifted him around. He fits everywhere.

"Sometimes his quickness and stick skills intimidate defenders and sometimes they hypnotize them."

Unfortunately for the Oilers, Gretzky's skating partners sometimes become entranced by his magic as well.

"Coming out of our end," Sather continued, "he always seems in position to take the pass and when he gets the puck, he knows where everybody is.

"Imagine what he would do if he had Orr passing the puck to him the way Phil (Esposito) did in Boston. What would he do if he had a Charlie Simmer on his line, or a Mike Bossy?"

Gretzky might not wind up as the greatest single-season goal-scorer in NHL annals, but surely either Simmer or Bossy would have. And Gretzky might have been in the 200-assist range.

But Gretzky doesn't have a Simmer or a Bossy or an Orr to aid him. And he manages just fine, thank you, with the help he gets.

◄ **One of 92 such celebrations.**

The Old Squeeze Play.

Game 7, vs. Flames at Calgary

Yes, Wayne Gretzky has a weakness. No, you won't find it on the ice.

Gretzky, by his own admission, is a lousy prognosticator.

"I picked us to finish 12th—no, 10th—last year and ended up way off," said Gretzky, whose club wound up 14th in the 21-team NHL, making the playoffs by a mere four points, even though Gretzky went on a record points binge. "The slow start is what hurt us as much as anything."

Another slow start, Gretzky knew, could send the Oilers right down the tubes again. And he was more than a little concerned when Edmonton was 3-3 after six games.

But a 5-4 win in this game had Gretzky feeling a lot better. He set up Paul Coffey's long-range goal early in the game and scored his fifth as Coffey returned the kindness in the second period. Low made 29 saves in a solid effort, shutting the door on the Flames after they pulled within 5-4 with 8½ minutes left.

"It was very important for us to get off to a good start," Gretzky explained. "The first 10 games are vitally important and we have to climb a steady pace over 80 games, peaking for the playoffs. Hopefully, we'll get the home-ice advantage in the playoffs so we don't have to travel so much."

Only three of the Oilers' nine playoff games in 1981 were at home.

As for the Smythe race, Gretzky predicted the Oilers would leap over Los Angeles, Calgary and Vancouver and win the division. Given his accuracy at such soothsaying in the past—and the fact that LA was fourth, Calgary seventh and Vancouver 12th overall the previous year—there were many clucking skeptics when Wayne made his picks.

"Sure, Los Angeles and Calgary are the teams to beat," he said. "Vancouver will be tough and I expect Colorado will improve as they go along. But we're shooting for the top. We may as well. There is no use going into a season unless you can finish first."

The Edmonton Oilers, even with the best player in the game, finishing first? Surely you jest.

"We'll see after 80 games," said Gretzky. "There isn't a guy on this team who doesn't think we'll be there."

Gretzky the Playmaker: always looking to pass.

Game 8, vs. Whalers at Edmonton

At this early point of the season, it was Messier who was tearing up the league, not Gretzky. The native of Edmonton, who is eight days older than Gretzky, was headed for a wonderful year himself after two seasons "of learning what NHL hockey is all about," he said.

Messier got his seventh goal of the young campaign 6:11 into the contest and the Oilers were on their way to a 5-2 walkover against Hartford. Gretzky was held scoreless for the second time in the first eight games of the season.

The win over the Whalers was Edmonton's first in more than a year when Gretzky didn't register a point. It also would be the last time in the 1981-82 season that the Oilers skated off with a victory while Gretzky skated off with no points.

With Gretzky having all kinds of problems with Hartford checkers, most notably Rick Meagher, the other Oiler centers picked up the slack. Matti Hagman had a goal and two assists and Unger also scored as Fuhr picked up his first NHL victory in the nets.

"We did a good job on Gretzky," said Whalers coach Larry Pleau. "But this game proved they're not a one-man team. They've got a lot of guys who can hurt you."

Hartford's Greg Miller, a goalie Gretzky makes a habit of victimizing, comes out on top here.

Mark Messier, who complemented Gretzky all season and fired 50 goals of his own.

Game 9, vs. Penguins at Edmonton

For once, Gretzky was not Edmonton's best center. Hagman, a native of Finland who flopped in a trial with the Boston Bruins, returned to Scandinavia for two years, then came back to the NHL to hook on with the Oilers, had possibly the best game of his North American career.

Hagman scored twice and set up two other goals as the Oilers bombed the Penguins 8-3. The Oilers connected on three of their first five shots against Pittsburgh goalie Paul Harrison, with Gretzky and Glenn Anderson each getting a goal.

Hagman's two goals gave him six in five games since returning from a broken foot. Gretzky was thrilled to see such a contribution.

"Matti loves to play and I know he must have been going through a rough time sitting out," said Gretzky. "He sure has come back with a vengeance. I know it helps the team and it helps me when another center is scoring."

Gretzky's goal came off some sloppy play in the Penguins' zone midway through the first period. He also assisted on a third-period tally by Coffey.

"I didn't think we did too badly against Gretzky," said Penguins defenseman Randy Carlyle. "We just couldn't stop anyone else. Maybe we concentrate so hard on stopping Gretzky that the rest of our play suffers.

"It seems natural that when he leaves the ice, somebody might let up. I'm not sure that's what happened to us, but it could."

Throughout his previous pro seasons—one in the WHA and two in the NHL—Gretzky had been a human dynamo. Sather relates a story which indicates why Gretzky is so special and why, when he is off the ice, the opposition has as much to fear as when he is on it.

"We were in a game in the WHA against Cincinnati," Sather recalled. "In the first period, Wayne made a terrible play in our end, a complete mistake, and he knew it. Any way, the other team scored and when Wayne came over to the bench, I think he understood what was going on, that I was about to bench him."

Gretzky credits Guy Lafleur as the man who got him to shoot more often.

Smoooooth.

Sather kept his young but somewhat undisciplined center off the ice for the entire second period. But, with Edmonton down 2-1, he sent Gretzky out for the third period.

"He could have pouted and sulked, but when I put him back in, he was like a tiger. He scored a hat trick and we won 5-2," Sather said. "That, to me, was the turning point of his career."

Ever since, Gretzky has been unstoppable. And early indications show he has lifted the Oilers close to that level.

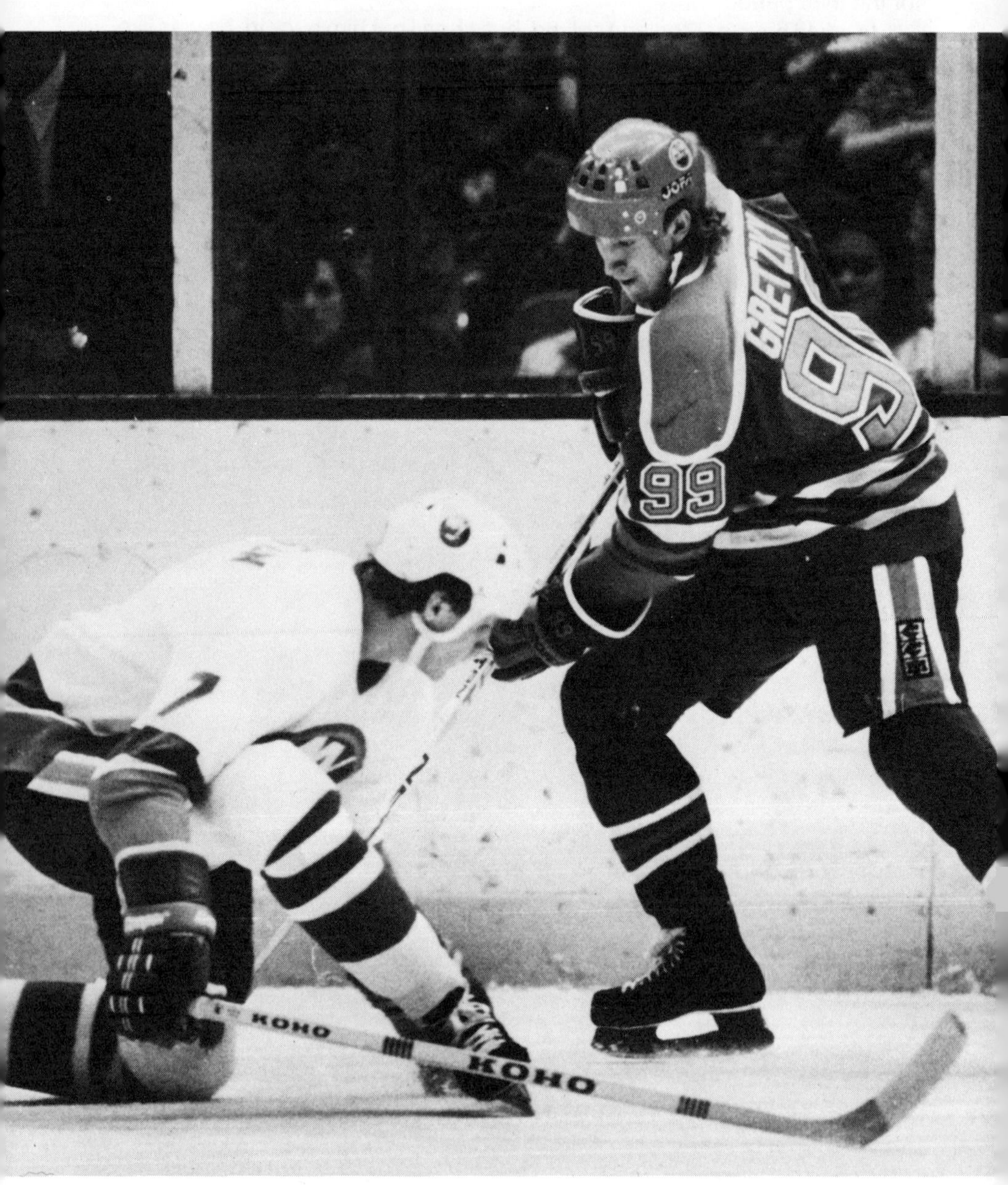

The old between-the-defenseman's legs trick.

Game 10, vs. Rockies at Colorado

As a measure of how bad the Colorado Rockies had become, it must be recalled that back in December 1980, they were beaten by the Winnipeg Jets. That victory snapped a record 30-game winless streak for the Jets, who were on their way to one of the worst seasons in sports history.

Ever since that defeat, the Rockies have headed in the exact opposite direction that the Oilers have taken.

Gretzky had just one assist against this ragtag bunch in the season opener. On this night, he had a goal and an assist but, considering what he was capable of doing to such a weak enemy, it was almost a moral victory for the outclassed Rockies.

Edmonton penetrated the sieve-like defense of the Rockies for 53 shots and Gretzky was involved in much of the action. He spurred many Oiler flurries but Colorado goalie Chico Resch was incredible as he kicked out 50 shots, many on breakaways and dead-on slappers.

"I had eight shots against Resch and I probably could have scored on six of them if he hadn't been so hot," said Gretzky. "We won, and that makes any game enjoyable. But watching Resch play like that was a treat, even though it was frustrating."

Imagine how Resch felt if Gretzky was feeling frustrated! Chico was the man all night and his comrades could do nothing to support his marvelous effort as the Oilers won 3-1.

"Some nights, a goalie's not going to be that sharp," said the garrulous Resch. "So the nights you are sharp, you hope it goes along with the team being sharp. I'll tell you, it's easier for me than for the guys up front. They were trying but it was one of those nights when you can't get untracked."

Resch stoned the Oilers in the first period, stopping 16 shots, including a couple on which Gretzky appeared to have plenty of room, only to see Chico come diving across the crease to make the stop.

But Messier got the Oilers started by finally solving Resch at 8:52 of the second period after Gretzky had been thwarted on a breakaway.

Colorado's Tapio Levo tied it on a power play; then Gretzky slid a 25-footer along the ice that Resch was screened on, and the Oilers were on top to stay. Messier scored again in the third period to ice it.

"This is the kind of game when you might expect to fatten up your statistics," said Coffey. "But when a goalie plays like that, you just feel lucky to get out with a win."

Game 11, vs. Islanders at New York
Game 12, vs. Rangers at New York

Gretzky and the Oilers slipped in and out of New York without much notice in late October. It was World Series time and, with the Yankees taking on the Dodgers in baseball's championships, hockey was shuttled to the inner pages of the sports sections in New York and to the final few seconds of sportscasts.

For those who were paying attention, though, it was a memorable two nights.

On Long Island, where Wayne played the best playoff game of his career in the Oilers' fifth-game quarterfinals victory over the Islanders the previous spring, the remarkable season he would have was nearly cut (or slashed, to be more accurate) short by Isles goalie Billy Smith.

Late in the second period, with the Oilers on top 3-1 on goals by Coffey, Risto Siltanen and Messier—Gretzky won a faceoff to set up Coffey's power-play goal—Wayne took the puck behind the Islander net. Knowing how dangerous Gretzky is from that spot—and certainly not feeling too chipper about being in a 1-3 hole—Smith decided to stop Gretzky without any help from his teammates. The goalie, known as "Battling Billy" for his willingness to mix it up and his hatchet jobs in protecting the crease—his crease—whacked Gretzky across the knee.

Gretzky went down as if his legs were chopped off; had Smith been yielding a sword, that's exactly what would have happened. Yet, no penalty was called and Smith acted as if he'd done nothing wrong.

Wayne limped off the ice and Sather, who was livid about Smith's not being penalized, feared the worst: a season-ending debilitation.

Without Wayne, the Oilers wilted and Wayne Merrick scored twice in the final period for a 4-3 Islander win. Sather, who was plenty disturbed by the loss, was seething after the game about the Smith-Gretzky incident.

"That was bull," said Sather. "Smith could have ended Wayne's career like that. I don't care who it is, Wayne Gretzky or a rookie up in his first NHL game, you don't do that. It's not the way this game's played.

"And for Smith to not even get a penalty out of it! We're going to send tapes of it to Montreal to the NHL office. Something's gotta be done about stuff like that. Smith's been doing it all his career. He thinks that's the way to protect himself and the net."

In defending himself—something he has gotten used to doing throughout his superb 10-year career—Smith claimed that he barely touched Gretzky and, if what he'd done was so bad, how come he didn't receive a penalty? Besides, added Smith, Gretzky "is no saint."

"He's a crybaby," said Smith. "He goes looking for the refs every time he gets touched. He might be a great player but you don't treat him any different than anybody else.

"Gretzky is known for scoring goals behind the net. Am I supposed to let him just score?

"He's a little _____ and he put on an act. Look, he's trying to beat me and I'm trying to beat him. If what I did was as terrible as he claimed, I would have gotten a penalty. Look at the films and you'll see what I mean."

The NHL office did and found no grounds for fining Smith. When Smith's comments were relayed to Gretzky, who had trouble walking as the Oilers left the Nassau Coliseum following the defeat, Wayne couldn't help but smile at the irony of Smith's words.

"I guess you have to consider the source," he said. "Billy should be talking about crybabies. All he did was complain and moan every day at the Team Canada camp (for the Canada Cup). He was trying to break up the team.

"Billy swung at me on purpose but I told people I didn't think he meant to hit me, just scare me off."

The Oilers listed Gretzky as "doubtful" for the game at Madison Square Garden the next night against the Rangers. But Gretzky provided a glimpse of another form of his greatness—superlative recuperative powers.

"Unless I couldn't walk or had a broken leg or something," he said, "I was going to play. It was a bit stiff and was bandaged up pretty well.

"In the first period, on the first couple of shifts, I was testing it. I wasn't sure if I could go all out and, if I couldn't, I was going to tell Slats (Sather). But it got looser and looser as the game went on."

And Gretzky got better and better. The Rangers grabbed a 3-1 margin after one period and, if not for the sparkling work of Fuhr, would have been blowing away the visitors by the time Gretzky turned matters around late in the second period.

Coffey lifted Edmonton within a goal on a power play earlier in the session; then the Rangers' Mikko Leinonen and Mark Pavelich were penalized.

"In that situation, when we're two men up, we try to make sure Wayne is handling the puck," said Coffey. "There's no one better with it anyway and, when you give us that much of an edge, Wayne's going to get us one (goal)."

Wayne got two to put the Oilers ahead 4-3. His eighth and ninth tallies of the season came 42 seconds apart in the final minute of the second period and catapulted Edmonton to a 5-3 decision over New York.

"Gretzky probably could have scored five goals tonight with all the chances we gave him," said Ranger defenseman Barry Beck. "We played stupid and you just don't do that against a Wayne Gretzky or a team which scores like the Oilers. They will jump all over your mistakes."

Gretzky did, earning two goals and two assists to match his biggest night of the early season.

How did Wayne enjoy the mini-trip to the Big Apple?

"The first part wasn't so good," he said. "But the second was fine."

Sather, who had calmed down—barely—over the "axe-swinging by Smith," as he put it, seemed in awe of his super center. The coach was wondering where Gretzky was hiding the "S" and the cape and the Clark Kent disguise.

"He's really chipped out of something special," said Sather, who was as impressed by Gretzky's bouncing back to play against the Rangers as he was by the four-point night. "I'm not sure he's mortal."

Game 13, vs. Nordiques at Edmonton

The Quebec Nordiques are the only NHL team with even the remotest chance of skating with the speedy Oilers. The Nordiques have become the game's "Flying Frenchmen," and they've adopted a "fire before you see the whites of their eyes, then fire again" approach.

Quebec was a most willing adversary in a game of shoot-em-up which featured 75 shots and 15 goals. The Oilers got 11 of them against goalies Daniel Bouchard and Michel Plasse, with Gretzky springing loose for his first heavy goal night of the season.

"When a team is willing to skate wide open with us like they did," he said, "then it's to our benefit. That's the kind of pace we like. It's the kind of pace they like. We had the guns tonight."

Gretzky was firing a howitzer. He tipped in a shot by Coffey in the second period, then opened fire for a third-period hat trick. Quebec coach Michel Bergeron put virtually all of his centers, plus left wing Alain Cote, on Gretzky without any luck.

"What can you do?" shrugged Bergeron. "We play our style because that is our best chance to win. Edmonton plays that style better than we do and they get 11 goals."

Up until this game, people spoke mainly of Wayne's passing skills. Just listen to what Unger, a veteran of 14 NHL campaigns, was saying.

"He sees everything and makes those soft little passes that look like they would be easy for a defenseman to pick off," noted Unger. "But he puts them right by the defenseman and, a second later, a teammate is there to pick it up. And most guys who handle the puck aren't good goal-scorers, too.

"But Wayne is shooting more and he has a terrific touch when he shoots.

"Every level he's reached just gives him that much more confidence. Everyone is always waiting for him to fall. OK, he had a great regular season and broke the (points) record last year. But everyone said, 'Let's see what he does against a good checking team like Montreal in the playoffs.'

"He blew them away. And he was great against the Islanders, too. And now he's better and the team being better helps too.

"So does Glen. He's the right coach for him. There's no special treatment, not that Wayne would ask for it. When Wayne does something wrong, he catches hell for it like everybody else. On a lot of teams, a player like that could run the club."

Instead, Gretzky was forcing other teams to run out of defenses. And the media to run out of superlatives.

And he was just getting started.

Game 14, vs. Maple Leafs at Edmonton

Just one month into the season and it was becoming clear: Wayne Gretzky had become a shooter.

Not that the premier passer and playmaker in hockey had turned his back on his teammates for the betterment of his own statistics. Gretzky still concentrated on a center's first job, which is to be the spur of the attack, even if he doesn't finish it off.

But, with two goals against Toronto, Gretzky was scoring at more than a goal-a-game pace. He would never dip below that pace again this season.

Gretzky tapped in a pass from Kurri six minutes into the game, helping the Oilers jump to a 3-1 lead after one period. He also scored into an empty net with four seconds remaining to clinch a 6-4 triumph.

Gretzky had added a dimension to his strategy of establishing a foothold behind the enemy net, then watching things develop and threading passes to his teammates in front. Opponents were wise to that part of his game, though they still couldn't do much to stop it. But Gretzky now was allowing the opposition to think he was headed behind the net and, instead, he was cutting for the slot.

"It opens up so many things when he goes behind the net," said right wing Dave Lumley, who soon would prosper from Gretzky's playmaking at a near-record clip. "You can see the whole ice, who is where, you can anticipate better. And the goalie has two areas of concentration—Wayne behind the net and anyone he might feed in front.

"The other team's guys don't want to be made fools of, so they back off. That's when Wayne is most dangerous.

"But if they don't back off—it looks to me like some teams are willing to chase him behind the net—he'll not go back there and, while the checkers are skating there, figuring that's where he's going to be, he's in front scoring."

"A lot of times I do things I've never done before," said Gretzky. "As I get older, I guess I get better at the things I can do. And I find more things to try doing. I know I can recognize situations better and adjust to them and that has to come from experience. There are some things a certain player can do better than others."

Like, in Gretzky's case, just about everything.

Game 15, vs. Rockies at Edmonton

Gretzky's three-game spurt came to an abrupt end against, of all teams, the weak Rockies. It was the second time in three meetings with Colorado that Wayne had performed below par.

The last time the Oilers met the miserable Rockies, Colorado goalie Chico Resch staged miracle after miracle just to keep it close and Edmonton wound up with a 3-1 decision in which Resch made 50 saves.

Edmonton once against exploited the inexperienced Colorado defense to fire shot after shot at Resch. And, once more, Chico sparkled, ending up with 46 saves. Thanks to Resch and a three-point game by rookie Tapio Levo of Finland, the Rockies skated to a surprising 5-4 win. They stormed back from a 4-1 deficit with just over 11 minutes left.

"Colorado played well, especially down the stretch, and we didn't," Gretzky said. "I don't know why we've had rough times with them except that Resch has been so tough.

"Any time you lose, you get frustrated. Professional athletes are paid to win and losing is no fun. I have a lot of pride as a professional athlete and I would be lying if I said I didn't care about my own contributions. If I score, it helps the team. If I don't I know there's a good chance we won't win.

"Resch made some fabulous saves. That kept them close; then we just let up. It shouldn't happen to a professional team but it does."

Gretzky and just about every other Oiler—including goalie Andy Moog, who would suffer most for the loss—played like so many Houdinis in the final period. They disappeared as the Rockies scored four times in 6½ minutes to steal the victory.

"That was embarrassing, especially in front of our own fans," said Sather, who promptly decided to scrap the three-man rotation in goal and go with Low and Fuhr. Moog was dispatched to the minor leagues, but Sather wouldn't admit he was singling out the goalie.

"Everyone was to blame," he snapped. "It was a total collapse."

Game 16
vs. Whalers at Hartford

The Hartford Whalers could blame bad luck, bad boards and Gretzky for not coming away with a victory over the Oilers, whom they outplayed but wound up tying 4-4.

The Whalers outshot Edmonton 43-35 and came from behind four times, the final goal off the stick of Blaine Stoughton with only 1:02 left.

Gretzky put on a pretty fair show in his only visit to the Hartford Civic Center; pity the Hartford fans, who got to see only the 16th game of the most incredible 80-game season anyone has ever managed. He scored early in the second period to put the Oilers on top 2-1, then assisted on Dave Hunter's goal, which made it 3-2 Edmonton in the third period.

After Rick Meagher lifted the Whalers into a 3-3 deadlock at 9:30, good fortune (and the puck) bounced Gretzky's way, as it would so often all season.

"I was just cruising around when the puck bounced off the boards right to me," he said. "It's not the kind of play you expect to see every day."

Gretzky put a quick shot into an open net with goalie Greg Millen well out of position, through no fault of his own.

"We've had trouble with those boards before but it never hurt us like that," said Whalers coach Larry Pleau.

"We were pretty discouraged after Gretzky got that goal," added Stoughton. "It's a tough way to fall behind late in a game, especially when you haven't made a mistake."

Stoughton matched Gretzky's output, however, scoring with a 30-foot wrist shot on a breakaway, just as he had earlier in the contest.

"We have a lot of character," said Millen. "We have the type of team that has to have enthusiasm every night and we've been getting it every night.

"We could've gotten down, given up, but we kept coming, even after Gretzky's goal. It was a very encouraging thing to tie it."

With a little help from their own boards, they probably would have had a win.

Game 17
vs. Bruins at Boston

Every superhero has his nemesis. Superman had Lex Luthor. Flash Gordon had Emperor Ming.

Wayne Gretzky has Steve Kasper.

Kasper is no crazed psycho, out to destroy the universe or mine all the gold on earth. He's a quiet, unassuming kid just out of his teens who makes a habit of shutting down the greatest scoring machine in hockey.

Kasper held Gretzky to a goal and three assists in their four meetings in the 1980-81 season, Kasper's rookie year. For that alone, Boston coach Gerry Cheevers claimed his young center deserved the Frank Selke Trophy as the NHL's best defensive forward.

"The kid is a dream," said Cheevers. "He's the kind of kid that would make you want to stay around coaching for a while. I think he should win the Selke this year because I don't think there is a better defensive player. We've put him head-to-head against some of the toughest people in the league and he's done a number on them. Not just Gretzky but Dionne, Bobby Smith, Stastny. He's handled all of them.

"And I think it's much tougher for a center to do a job covering someone than it is for a wing."

The Selke award, which Kasper would win in 1981-82, went to Bob Gainey in its first four years of existence. But no matter how well Gainey performed last season, Kasper grabbed all the attention, headlines and writers' votes by his terrific work against Gretzky for a second straight season.

The Oilers came to Boston with Gretzky already on a two-points-a-game pace. He would get his two points in the Garden, assisting on a pair of power-play goals. But the Bruins already held a 3-1 lead before Gretzky set up Anderson early in the third period. Boston scored again before Gretzky and Coffey combined to spring Hagman.

It was a frustrating night for the Edmonton players because they had allowed Boston to get a jump and never got untracked in the first 40 minutes. When they came alive in the last period, it was too late.

Not surprisingly, the Bruins were throwing all the credit to Kasper, who assisted on Boston's opening goal. But scoring, especially against the Oilers, isn't Kasper's job, and his shadowing of Gretzky was the most significant contribution he made. This was one Kasper the Ghost on Gretzky's back which Wayne didn't find at all friendly.

"Guys like Gretzky carry the scoring load for Edmonton, just like the other guys Steve checks," said Peter McNab, a veteran Bruins center. "You figure if you take them out of their offense, you take their team out of the game.

"Steve Kasper has done that. He has unusual poise and concentration for someone his age, to do the job he's been asked to do. You see some guys try it and they're OK for about a period and a half. All of a sudden they start to lose the concentration a little bit and, boom, they give up a goal. They try to make up for it and it's another goal.

"Steve never lets up. He stays after them the whole game and he doesn't get flustered."

Gretzky didn't seem particularly flustered about the Oilers' bad night in Beantown. He even admitted to admiring Kasper's style.

"He plays hard and clean and if a guy stops me or anyone else playing that way, there are no complaints," Gretzky said. "I don't know why he does well against me and against us. If I did, he wouldn't do well any more, would he?"

Gretzky was wearing a huge smile as he said that. He could be comfortable in the knowledge that there is just one Steve Kasper and that everyone else in the NHL who was assigned to shadow him had most of the time disappeared as Gretzky skated freely and chalked up points with ease. They disappeared like, well, like a ghost.

Game 18
vs. Islanders at New York

Due to an unfortunate display of poor scheduling, Gretzky and the Oilers made their final trip to the media capital of the U.S. long before Wayne was threatening to demolish the record books.

Just two weeks earlier, Edmonton made a similar trip to New York, losing to the Islanders 4-3 in a game that saw Isles' goalie Billy Smith chop Gretzky in the knee with his stick. The next night, the Oilers, with Gretzky playing despite the discomfort in his leg, beat the Rangers 5-3. Gretzky had two goals and two assists while doing his impersonation of Chester from the old "Gunsmoke" series (surely you remember the gimpy-legged character played by Dennis Weaver).

Smith was still in a foul mood about the run-in with Gretzky. He continued to claim that Wayne wasn't hurt and was putting on an act.

"I didn't even know who it was until he came around in front and laid there like a dead whale," said Smith. "How was I to know he had a boo-boo and I hit it?

"I went through a lot of crap about it. Because of the press, I was persecuted about it. But I swung while I was looking straight out in front of the net. I hit something but I couldn't have been swinging any higher than the kneecap.

"If I had hit him anywhere up here (in the groin), OK, then crucify me," Smith added. "But the kneecap? The films show what I mean."

Gretzky certainly would prefer to watch the films of his team's play in its second visit to Nassau Coliseum. Gretzky had a goal and three assists as the Oilers rallied from 4-1 and 5-3 deficits to escape with a 5-5 tie.

Most satisfyingly, Gretzky beat Islanders' goalie Rollie Melanson—Smith sat this one out—with only 39 seconds left to earn the tie.

"We allowed them to dictate the pace, which was fast and furious," said Islanders coach Al Arbour. "It was stupid for us to do, but we got caught up in a real shootout and that's what the Oilers like best."

Indeed, the teams combined for 73 shots on goal, with Fuhr making 35 saves.

"Once it started to get wide open, I knew we had a chance," Gretzky said. "The Islanders like to keep it tight but we proved tonight that we can set the pace even against the best teams."

It was a game to remember because the three best players in the NHL all had special nights. Aside from Gretzky, New York's Mike Bossy—the league's premier goal-scorer until Gretzky began shooting more—also had a goal and three assists, while his linemate, center Bryan Trottier, had two goals and an assist.

"When there are players in the NHL like Bossy and Trottier, they should be showcased," said Gretzky. "It's what hockey is all about. We need to promote our people who are good, clean players.

"You look at beer commercials and what do they show? They just show guys fighting, not the way hockey is. The people in the league work overtime to clean up the image. Then a guy goes on nationwide television and says all we have is goons and it has to be cleaned up.

"There are a lot more players like Bossy and Trottier who they should look at."

Of course, he could have added the name "Gretzky" to the list.

Game 19
vs. Rangers at New York

There are two ways to look at the kind of trip the Oilers made to New York. If you are coaching the Rangers, however, you see only the bad side.

Why? Just look at the results.

"They come in and play out at the Island and it gets them up for us the next night," complained Rangers' coach Herb Brooks. "Look, they're a pretty fair team but they got an advantage on both trips here because they played the Islanders first."

Actually, the Oilers probably would have preferred to reverse the order of games in New York, even though they beat the Rangers a second straight time 5-3 at Madison Square Garden after playing the night before on Long Island.

A two-day journey to the Big Apple to play hockey isn't much of a treat these days, with the Islanders right at the top of the pack and the Rangers rapidly moving towards the peak under the astute Brooks. Games on Long Island tend to take a lot out of a club as it strives just to keep up with the potent Islanders. If anything, those visitors should be ripe for the Rangers.

But the scores indicate otherwise, as Brooks suggested.

Gretzky and Lumley each had a goal and two assists in subduing the Rangers, who wilted in the third period after rookie defenseman Reijo Ruotsalainen tied it at 2:07. Lumley untied it 27 seconds later and then assisted on Hunter's empty-net goal to clinch it.

Many of the Rangers were ready to offer their theories on what makes Gretzky so good. None of them used a description below "great."

"When I play the game, I have a certain way of seeing the rink, the players and the puck," said Dave Silk, who played for Brooks on the gold medal-winning 1980 U.S. Olympic team.

"There is a certain way I anticipate the play. I'd like to play one game with Gretzky's head.

"He sees the game different from anyone else. He's only 20, so you can't chalk it up to experience. It's a knack and an amazing one."

Added Mark Pavelich, another Olympian now with the Rangers, "It's as if he sees the game from the stands. He sees it like you would from the best seat in the house. He sees every play developing."

Ranger defenseman Carol Vadnais spoke of Gretzky's passing, which had been the most polished part of his game until now.

"He seems to be lobbing the puck," said Vadnais. "He's not hitting sticks. He lobs it soft and the guy just skates into it."

Rookie goalie Steve Weeks had faced Gretzky for the first time. It didn't take long for Weeks to recognize Gretzky's skills.

"He's unbelievably tricky," Weeks said. "You have to be aware of where he is. You hope the rest of the guys are keeping track of him all the time because you can't be watching one guy. But if you did try that, he'd be the one you had to watch.

"He can do so much from behind the net, which isn't a place you usually watch guys real close. Him you watch. But he's smart. He's going to do the opposite of what you think.

"It's scary because sometimes you get the feeling he knows what you're thinking and what you're planning to do. And you know when it's him coming down at you but there's nothing special you can do."

Defenseman Dave Maloney, who was victimized on Lumley's game-winner, couldn't believe how quickly Gretzky gets back into the flow.

"On that fourth goal, I got him in the corner," said Maloney. "I took him off the puck and out of the play. The next thing I know, he's got it again and throws it through five guys to Lumley and they score."

Gretzky had given a fair indication on the ice of what lay ahead for him. In the dressing room, he offered a clear explanation of why it was to happen.

"I'm doing things I've never done before," he said. "I'm staying in front of the net more, not skating behind it so much. It's a change of pace and I can shoot at the net more. Teams know I go behind the net and they practice against it.

"When I was with Team Canada, my linemates were Gil Perreault and Guy Lafleur. They were the ones who said I should shoot more."

Sather figured Gretzky's change of style was a sign of his maturing.

"Before, he'd sit behind the net with the pick and make all those nice passes for scores," Sather said."Teams started to get wise, even though they couldn't stop him. Now he's coming out from behind and getting in position to shoot himself.

"We told him he'd have to spend less time behind the net and he knew it. But he's still going through that growing up stage."

Gretzky was asked what, at this early junction of the season, were his objectives for the rest of the year. His pace at this point was a modest goal-a-game—modest in light of what was ahead.

"I'd like to score 50 goals in 50 games, like Mike Bossy," he said. "I'd like to break it but I don't want to come right out and say I'm going for this or that. Why put on that added pressure?"

Instead, he applies the added pressure to the opposition every night. Maloney knows what that's like.

"The only thing deceptive about him is, no matter how high you estimate him, he's better than what you think," said Maloney. "He's the smartest player in the world and the most exciting and the best. I wish he was a Ranger."

Nineteen other teams wish they had a No. 99 in their lineup, too.

"Yeah," added Maloney. "Maybe we can incorporate him and sell shares. Even a piece of the rock is better than none at all."

Game 20, vs. Blues at St. Louis

For the first time this season, the two most successful and valuable players from the 1980-81 season met.

Gretzky, of course, was coming off his record-setting year as well as a spectacular playoff. St. Louis goaltender Mike Liut had been the only player in the NHL who came close to challenging Gretzky's overall achievements last season.

Working behind a leaky defense, Liut had managed a 33-14-13 record and a 3.34 goals-against average. He appeared in 61 of the Blues' 80 games and was the only man to get any solid support in chasing Gretzky for the Hart Trophy as the league's MVP.

Unlike Gretzky, Liut faltered in the playoffs, looking overworked from his busy regular season. And, in direct contrast to Gretzky, Liut was off to an indifferent start this season, as were the Blues.

St. Louis had shocked hockey fans by rising from mediocrity to near the top of the league standings in 1980-81, much as Edmonton would do this season. But the Blues, perhaps over-confident after such prosperity, had sunk back to the lower echelons of the NHL, where they would stay throughout the season.

"We're having problems all over the ice," said coach Red Berenson, the NHL's coach of the year the previous season. "When our offense works, our defense is at fault. When we shut down the other team, we can't score."

It was more of the same against the Oilers, who threw 40 shots at Liut and skated off with a 5-1 verdict. Gretzky scored the final two goals, putting him just above the goal-a-game clip with 21 in 20.

"I'm going to have to pinch myself to see if I'm real," he said after winning a faceoff and ripping the puck past Liut to make it 4-1, then tapping home a

NORTHLAND
NORTHLAND
99

GRETZKY
99
NORTHLAND

▲

Not even Mike Liut, the star goalie for the St. Louis Blues, has a chance when Gretzky gets this free . . . and this close.

◄

loose puck from just outside the crease to close out the scoring. "I'd like to think we can keep up this pace and that I can keep scoring like this."

Berenson had no doubts about Gretzky keeping it up.

"I'm convinced he's the greatest player in the game and, at his age, that's phenomenal," said Berenson. "He's not the greatest goal-scorer and he isn't the greatest skater, although he is deceptive.

"His greatness lies in the fact he'll do things nobody else will. He has that second and third level depth perception of what is taking place within the framework of the game.

"Most people in the NHL are aware of the initial play as it's happening. Others . . . the outstanding players . . . see the level beyond the initial play.

"But Gretzky constantly goes beyond that second level. He has the ability to make poor players look great. Anything he does, any numbers he puts up there, wouldn't surprise me. He's that far ahead of everyone else."

Game 21, vs. North Stars at Minnesota

By not scoring a point in a 2-2 tie with Minnesota, Gretzky ensured that he would not dominate every team in every building in the league. This was the Oilers' only trip to the Met Center and it would wind up as the only NHL arena in which Gretzky did not score at least one point during his majestic season.

Considering what he would do later this season to the North Stars, it was surprising that Wayne could be blanked all night by Minnesota. But the Oilers didn't exactly sparkle and the game was controlled by a pair of kid goalies. Fuhr, who was 19, stopped 24 shots. Don Beaupre, the puck-stopping phenom of 1980-81, and a year and two days older than Fuhr, made 32 saves.

This would be the only game in a span of 24 in which Gretzky did not get a point. For the next five weeks, from late fall into the dead of winter, Gretzky would sizzle, scoring at least a point every night.

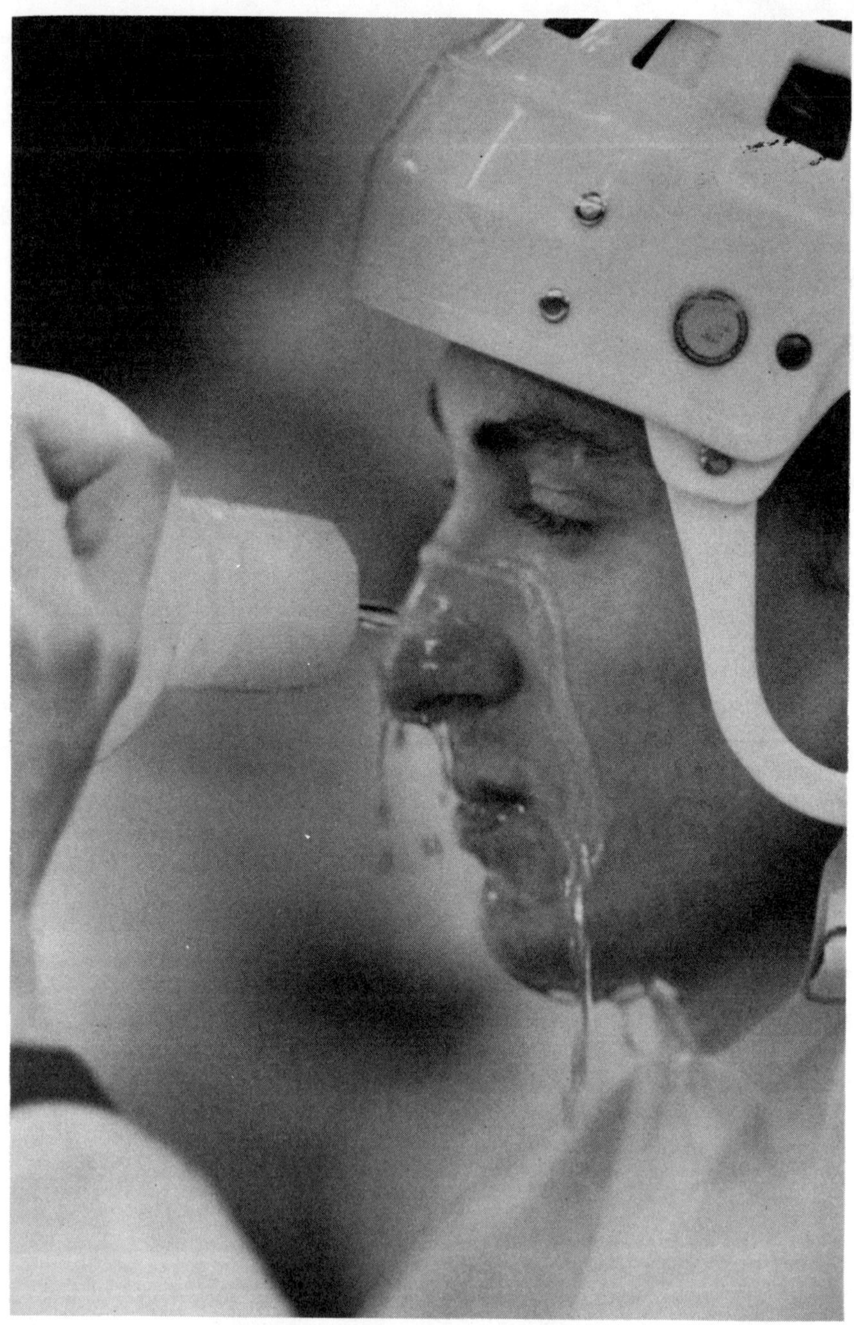

Gretzky doesn't always hit his target.

Game 22, vs. Canucks at Edmonton

Gretzky would score twice and set up two goals in an 8-3 rout of Vancouver, but it was a tally he had nothing to do with that was most significant in this game.

Just 1:27 into the contest, Lumley popped the puck over Canucks goalie Richard Brodeur. It was only the second goal of the season for Lumley, who had been in Sather's doghouse for more than a season.

But, for the 27-year-old right wing, it was the beginning of a joy ride he probably never dreamed of making. For the next 11 games, carrying through nearly a month, Lumley would get at least one goal.

Gretzky did assist on Lumley's second goal of the night and Lumley assisted on both of Wayne's goals.

Eleven minutes into the game, the Oilers led 4-0 and they coasted behind Fuhr the rest of the way. The Canucks, usually a tight-checking, disciplined club, had opted for a freewheeling game with the Oilers. The teams combined for 85 shots, with Brodeur stopping 33 and Fuhr making 41 saves, the most of his short professional career.

Canucks coach Harry Neale noticed the standout play of Fuhr but was more expansive on Gretzky's virtues following the wipeout.

"He's a mile-and-a-half ahead of everybody else," said Neale. "He doesn't look like he's skating . . . but he never gets caught. And he's so slippery.

"He's like a good soccer player who kicks the ball to an opening nobody else sees. But when the ball gets there, someone's there and kicks it in. It's uncanny.

"With Lumley and Dave Semenko on his line—their job is to stop the puck from spinning and get it to lie flat for Gretzky—he gets to make them look like All-Stars.

"Semenko has a great effect on that team," added Neale, who later in the season would get a first-hand look at just how important Semenko could be. "One time Gerry Minor (a Canucks' center) shoved Gretzky in the face and Semenko came off the bench after him. Semenko was thrown out and our guys grew a foot-and-a-half and 50 pounds.

"You're not allowed to touch Gretzky, cleanly or not, or Semenko challenges you. I've seen Gretzky nod his head, as if he's saying, 'Take care of this guy,' and Semenko is right on the case.

"Gretzky gets to take all kind of liberties and he's got a squad of guys to protect him."

And if he didn't have those protectors, what would happen? If Gretzky had an opponent following him around all evening, step for step, and roughing up the star as often as possible? What then, Harry?

"Sometimes you put a man right on him," said Neale, "and he only gets four goals."

Game 23, vs. Red Wings at Edmonton

The third hat trick of Anderson's career paced the Oilers over Detroit 8-4. Gretzky registered a goal and an assist but was far more interested in Anderson's contributions.

"Is there anyone who enjoys playing the game more than Glenn Anderson?" Gretzky asked about the former Canadian Olympic team star. "He's a pleasure to play with and a pleasure to watch. He hustles every minute and he has a good time at it."

It was becoming evident that when the Oilers were in high gear, few teams could stop them, or even hope to slow them down. They'd already scored 120 goals in 23 games, including the 11-goal breakout against Quebec, four eight-goal games and two sevens.

Everyone was getting involved. Only Anderson and Gretzky had scored hat tricks thus far, but Messier and Hagman each had three two-goal contests, Kurri had a pair of them and Pat Hughes, Lumley, Unger and Gallighen had a two tally night apiece.

That's aside from Gretzky's four-goal explosion and five two-goal games.

Lumley, Hagman, Anderson, Kurri, Siltanen and, naturally, Gretzky all had games with at least four points.

This was no one-man team.

"We'll get in situations where we go up 4-1 or more, and the other team can't concentrate on one line," analyzed Gretzky. "With Matti, Mark, Andy and a lot of the other guys scoring, it makes all of us more effective."

The scores would continue to soar.

Don't forget your stick, Wayne.

Mark Howe of Team USA attempts to stop Wayne Gretzky.

Game 24, vs. Kings at Edmonton

"I never used to think about what I'll do next," Gretzky asserted. "But, lately, I've started to. If I'm doing the same thing in 10 years that I'm doing now, will people say that I haven't improved? That I've gone backwards or leveled out?

"Whatever job you have or whatever thing you're doing, if it's water skiing, playing baseball, your attitude has to always be to improve. Gordie Howe showed it. Every year, he went in and thought he had to do better and that set him apart.

"Somewhere down the road you get to a line where it's a matter of trying to maintain your consistency. I don't think I've reached that yet."

While Gretzky pondered the future, he was making a mockery of the present NHL schedule. Against the defense-poor Kings, he struck for four goals and an assist in an 11-4 romp.

Gretzky scored in all manners on this night and, if he had so chosen, probably could have had a few more goals. Instead, he settled for four—no glutton he—for the second time this season.

Once again, the Oilers broke to a 3-0 edge in the first period, with Gretzky connecting twice, including a power-play goal off a fine feed from Anderson.

He got another power-play goal in the second period, circling in the Kings' zone while the point men controlled the puck, then breaking for paydirt and beating netminder Jim Rutherford after getting the puck from defenseman Doug Hicks.

His final goal of the night came just as a penalty to Marc Habscheid, a youngster up from juniors for a short trial, was expiring.

"Wayne is changing the whole game of hockey around," said Kings center Marcel Dionne, who won the scoring title in 1979-80 by virtue of scoring more goals (53 to 51) than Gretzky; each had 137 points. "Watch kids coming up. They'll be playing a different game. They'll be trying to move the puck the way he does."

Trying. But nobody does it like Gretzky.

"He's amazing," added Dionne. "You have to think he'll be setting all kinds of records every year, the way he's going. I don't know who's going to win the scoring title again, other than him, for a long time."

The five-point outburst gave Gretzky 28 goals and 55 points in 24 games. He was just shy of a 200-point pace.

"I said before the season if anyone is ever going to get 200, it would be last year, this or next," he admitted. "The league is going through a transition right now with so many young players. They'll be better and tougher (and harder to score against) in the next couple of years.

"I think 200 is realistic. I don't think it's impossible. The fans like to see goals, the teams and players are more offensive-minded and the coaches are opening up things a lot more.

"Just look at us. We have a bunch of young players who just keep skating and skating. After a while, we just wear down the defenses."

When they come up against a well-worn defense like LA's, it means double figures for the team and monster nights for Gretzky.

Game 25, vs. Black Hawks at Edmonton

For Shakespeare, the play was the thing. For Gretzky, it's the game.

Wayne put on another show as the Oilers humbled Chicago 8-1. He scored twice and set up three more goals for his second consecutive five-point night.

Gretzky won a faceoff which led to a power-play goal by Semenko early in the contest, then fed Hicks for a tally at 15:11 as Edmonton took a 3-0 edge. That lead soared to 5-1 before Gretzky made the third period a personal showcase. He scored No. 29 only 29 seconds into the session on a nice feed from Lumley, then put in his 30th goal at 15:00. To conclude matters, Gretzky and Semenko assisted on a goal by Lumley, the fourth straight game in which the one-time member of Sather's doghouse had put the puck home.

Afterwards, Gretzky was asked how much fun he was having, considering the team's success—they were 16-6-3—and his own incredible scoring pace—2.4 points and 1.2 goals a game.

"The only way I'd enjoy it more," he said, "was if, instead of 80 games, and 80 practices, we had 160 games and no practices."

But—and all you cliche haters are advised to duck here—as Wayne understands, practice makes perfect.

"I've practiced so long, so many times, that nothing can happen that I haven't seen before," he claimed. "It's not so much anticipation as experience. A lot of people think what I do is instinct. But it isn't. Nobody would ever say a doctor had learned his profession by instinct.

"Well, I've learned. I've spent almost as much time studying hockey as a med student puts into studying medicine."

Wayne's father was the catalyst in his learning the importance of practice.

"He once told me that instead of practicing, I could be out working," Wayne recalled. "I went right back to practicing."

"He practiced everything for hours," said Walter Gretzky, who built a rink in the backyard of the Gretzky home in Brantford. "How many kids would do that when the temperature was minus-15? We had to bring him in. When his fingers and toes started to thaw, he would scream blue murder."

According to Sather, all that practice hasn't made Gretzky a master of the classic style of playing hockey. But that matters little when the results are so large.

"Wayne does some things that are technically incorrect," said Sather. "He'll turn up in places where he shouldn't be. But we allow it; how can you tamper with his God-given talent?"

Not all of it is purely talent. It's the way Wayne applies that talent.

"The thing I drilled most into Wayne was concentration," said his father. "That's what gives him his edge today. He puts so much thought into what he's doing. He doesn't just chase the puck around. He goes to where the puck is going to be."

And, when he gets there, he sends the puck where it's supposed to be, which is why through 25 games, he had 30 goals and 60 points.

Game 26, vs. Jets at Winnipeg

There's no love lost for Edmonton in Winnipeg, the eastern-most of Canada's frontier towns. But the folks at the Winnipeg Arena must have cringed when the Oilers were introduced as the "Edmonton Eskimos."

First off, there was no reason to give the Oilers extra incentive to beat up on the Jets, who had won the teams' only matchup so far this season. While the Jets were a vastly improved club, they weren't close to being in the Oilers' class. And, secondly, the Eskimos have dominated the Canadian Football League for years. Who needs another Edmonton juggernaut?

Which is exactly what the sellout crowd of 15,756 witnessed. The Oilers were as awesome as the Eskimos had ever been, building a 6-0 margin and easing to a 10-2 shellacking of the Jets.

Coffey had two goals and three assists and Gretzky a goal and three assists to pace the bombardment of the Jets, whose goalie, Ed Staniowski, stopped only 18 shots.

"Tonight we had our first sellout and laid a giant egg," said Jets coach Tom Watt. "It almost makes a guy wish he was back teaching English."

The other coach, Sather, was thrilled with what he had seen.

"The best team game of the year," he boasted. "When you talk about total team efforts, that's what you mean. That kind of game from everyone."

Gretzky started the rout by converting a breakaway at 9:44. He helped Hunter make it 5-0 at 1:04 of the second period, then dropped a pass to Hughes, who sent a slapshot by Staniowski for 7-2. Gretzky's final assist was a perfect setup that Semenko knocked in at the goalmouth just 37 seconds into the third period.

"After my goal, I reverted to playmaking," Gretzky noted with a grin.

Anderson's goal late in the third period should have been the hint Winnipeg needed that it was the Oilers' night. Defenseman Bryan Maxwell tripped Anderson, who then slid into the net. Staniowski jumped up to avoid being hit by Anderson and the puck traveled into the net right along with Andy.

"I was annoyed he jumped," said Anderson. "I thought he'd protect me. I was worried about sliding into the post.

"Until I saw the puck in the net and the light on."

The Edmonton Eskimos, er, Oilers strike again.

Game 27, vs. Canadiens at Montreal

La Belle Province would not be kind to the Oilers all season. On this, their first trip to Quebec, they would tie the Canadiens 3-3 at the same Montreal Forum where they'd begun their monumental playoff upset the previous spring. And, in the Colisee in Quebec City, Edmonton and Quebec would stage one of the wildest games in a wild NHL season. The Nordiques wound up on top 9-8 in that shootout.

Montreal's hockey fans—which means just about everyone in that city and its environs—anxiously awaited the return of Gretzky and company. The December 1 matchup was touted in the press as the most anticipated hockey game in Montreal since the seventh game of the 1979 Stanley Cup semifinals against Boston. Scalpers were getting as much as $80 per ticket.

It was not just another game for the Oilers, either. They were eager to prove something.

"Beating the Canadiens last year was a big thrill for all of us," said defenseman Kevin Lowe. "This game is a chance to show it was no fluke."

A crowd of 18,094 showed up, hopeful of seeing Gretzky continue his points onslaught while the Canadiens racked up enough goals to win. Wayne had become as big a hero as any athlete in Canada, even in Montreal and regardless of how he'd devastated Les Canadiens a few months before.

Midway through the opening period, Montreal got the jump when Pierre Larouche beat Fuhr, who admittedly was a bit nervous in his first start at the holiest temple in hockey. But Hunter got it back 3:10 later, taking a pass from Gretzky and putting the puck through the pads of Canadiens' goalie Richard Sevigny. The fact that Rod Langway, one of the NHL's best defensemen, was all over him, committing all kinds of mayhem, didn't bother Hunter.

Late in the second period, Montreal pulled ahead once more, this time on Keith Acton's tip-in of Langway's shot. And it took Edmonton less than three minutes to knot it again. Gretzky found Hunter and hit him with a pass that Hunter quickly fed to Anderson near the goal. Andy tipped it in.

Then it was the Oilers' turn to grab a lead, with Lumley converting Gretzky's pass with a 35-footer.

"I was going to go around (Montreal defenseman Brian) Engblom but he just kept backing up," said Lumley. "I saw this open strip of net and no goalie, so I shot. It was silent but deadly . . . it didn't make a sound."

The lead was short-lived as Mark Napier scored 2:20 after Lumley. The Canadiens continued to press Fuhr, who stood tall and firm with 35 saves, including 15 in the last period. The rookie goalie was sensational, being fooled only when Napier, with defenseman Mike Forbes covering him like a bad smell, skated out from the side of the net and jammed the puck past Fuhr.

"He certainly seems to come up with the big save," Napier said of Fuhr. "He sure as hell isn't hurting them."

Gretzky had hurt the Canadiens in this game but nowhere near as much as he did in the playoffs. He helped set up all three Edmonton goals but couldn't manage any good scoring opportunities for himself.

"They checked me real well," he said, giving credit to people like Doug Risebrough. "I had three shots on goal but none were really good ones, no tough saves for him. Those things are going to happen. They're such a good defensive team.

"You can't score every game."

It was the first time in six games that Gretzky failed to get a goal. But he impressed everyone with his three assists and general rink manner.

"Gretzky is the best and he proved it against us," said Sevigny, the same netminder who'd made the unfortunate comments last spring that Guy Lafleur would "put Gretzky in his back pocket." Instead, Gretzky knocked the Canadiens through the side pocket, off the table and clear out of the building.

"What player can have 64 points in only 28 games," added Sevigny.

Defenseman Robert Picard had another question. Does Gretzky have a bonus for 50 (goals) before Christmas? he wondered.

"Our game plan was to neutralize Gretzky if we can," said Guy Lapointe, who was then playing defense for Montreal. "We actually did a good job on him. But he made some unbelievable plays anyway."

Hunter, who registered a goal and two assists and now had nine goals—his previous season high was 12—put it all in perspective for the Oilers.

"Playing with the Great One, how can you not pick up points?"

WAYNE GRETZKY IS . . .

POETRY IN MOTION

EXCITING
CCM

A SCORING MACHINE

A RECORD BREAKER

A CHARMER

A FAN

A WINNER

Game 28, vs. Nordiques at Quebec City

The schedule called for a short hop to Quebec City for a game the next night with Les Nordiques. Fast becoming one of the most exciting teams in the NHL—and the darlings of fans throughout the province—the Nordiques were a dangerous foe. Sather feared a shootout after the tight play in Montreal.

"The game in Montreal was old-time hockey," he said. "They checked us so closely we never got a chance to open up. I think my players are itching to open it up against Quebec."

There would be plenty of wide-open play in the Colisee, enough to satisfy the most offense-minded of players. Both teams played "Damn the Torpedoes" hockey and Quebec wound up on the long end of a 9-8 score.

9-8 would indicate that Gretzky went hog wild. But he remained in the chorus as Messier connected three times and Hughes scored twice. Wayne notched two assists.

Center stage belonged to pesky Dale Hunter, Dave's brother and one of the few fearsome Nordiques: Dale would just as soon give you an extra jab with his stick as control the puck. He scored three times against Low and the Stastny brothers combined for four goals in the second period, with Peter—who often was paired against Gretzky at center—getting two of those tallies.

Gretzky assisted on Siltanen's power-play goal in the middle period and Messier's 20th of the season in the third.

The highlight of the night for Edmonton was Lumley's ninth goal of the season and seventh in as many games. After breaking in alone on Quebec goalie Daniel Bouchard, Lumley was dumped by Bouchard, prompting a penalty shot. He cleanly beat Bouchard with the shot.

That was the only solace the somber Oilers could get from their trip to Quebec City. Low, who stopped only 23 of 32 shots, understood what happened.

"Eight goals should have been enough to win," he said. "We didn't have much defense or goaltending out there. It stunk."

Game 29, vs. Canucks at Edmonton

Gretzky's goal-scoring drought would reach four games as the Canucks blanked him twice in a row. But he picked up five assists in the two games to give him 16 in the last six outings.

"As long as I'm helping the team and other guys are scoring," said Gretzky, "then I'm satisfied. A center is paid to be a playmaker and that's what I've been doing. And we're not losing."

Indeed, the two contests with Vancouver—a 7-3 home-ice win and a 3-3 tie on the West Coast—began a seven-game string without a loss.

The 7-3 victory was sparked by Semenko, the lumbering left wing whose main job is to protect Gretzky from other NHL players of Semenko's ilk. Harry Neale, who was serving as Canucks coach (he would relinquish the role late in the season and throughout the playoffs to assistant Roger Neilson), once had remarked that Semenko looked like he should be carrying ice, not skating on it. But even a harsh critic such as Neale was impressed by the Semenko he saw this night.

"He's a very valuable guy," said Neale, who watched the 6-3, 200-pound Semenko score twice. "He gets enough goals to keep him happy and he's a physical threat that every team needs."

Trailing 2-1 after a period, the Oilers blew it open with six straight goals. The first three came in a 6½-minute span of the second period and Semenko canned two of them.

At 2:03, he got his fourth goal of the season and, at 9:01, he took a pass from Gretzky and tapped in a short shot.

Then Semenko got back to more familiar territory: the penalty box.

Late in the period, Semenko spotted Vancouver's Tiger Williams taking liberties with Gretzky.

"I thought he took a run at Gretzky," said Semenko. "He gave me a little shove; then the linesman (Randy Mitton) got in the way. I thought I might as well finish it off."

Since Semenko had effectively started the Oilers in the contest, his "finishing it off" seemed appropriate.

"Semenko was the fire that got us going," said assistant coach Ted Green. "He set up our first goal with his hitting, scored two of his own and took care of Tiger in a fight. After that, the Canucks weren't the same team."

Gretzky's other assists came on Lumley's first-period goal, which made it eight straight games in which Lumley had registered a goal, and on Coffey's power-play blast in the third stanza.

Game 30, vs. Canucks at Vancouver

The next night in Vancouver, Lumley got two more goals to reach nine in a row. Gretzky assisted on one of those and on Mike Forbes' first NHL goal.

"I'm not worried about not getting the goals as long as I'm getting the chances," Gretzky said. "I hit the post on a breakaway and I had five shots, so I'm in there plugging at it."

After a scoreless first period, the Canucks' Harold Snepsts snuck one by Fuhr a minute into the second period.

"I think Fuhr thought Thomas Gradin was going to deflect it but it just kept going along the ice and into the net," said Snepsts.

Lumley tied it three minutes later after a memorable play by Gretzky. Wayne stole the puck from Vancouver defenseman Rick Lanz, stripping it right off his stick, and then delivered it to Semenko. He relayed to a cutting Lumley alone in front of Canucks goalie Glen Hanlon, who had no chance to stop Lumley.

Then it was Forbes' turn. "The goalie must have read I never scored," said the rookie defenseman, "and he felt sorry for me."

Lumley made it 3-1 at 5:56 of the third period, walking out of the corner to beat Hanlon on the glove side.

"At that point," said Sather, "it seemed like we had it. But our guys made a lot of mistakes in the last five minutes. They were tired. I looked on the bench and some guys weren't even sweating. They had nothing left."

Which wasn't surprising since the Oilers hadn't had more than two straight off days at any time since November 7 and this was December 5. They had been playing every other night almost consistently for a month, except for a two-day respite before their last meeting with Vancouver on November 21.

Gradin brought the Canucks within a goal with 5:40 to go, backhanding the puck over a fallen Fuhr. Two minutes later, Darcy Rota lifted Vancouver into the 3-3 deadlock.

"I completed a rink-length rush and fired into the upper corner," joked Rota. "Actually, it looked like Fuhr had it stopped at first and then it trickled under him."

Rota had lunged for a loose puck and barely touched it, with the puck sneaking under Fuhr.

"It was between my legs and I thought I had it," said Fuhr. "Then I heard the crowd cheering."

Rota wasn't being particular about how he scored.

"It doesn't matter if they won't win any awards," he said. "I'll take 'em anyway I can get 'em."

And the Canucks were glad to have the point for the tie.

"The Oilers are just eating up teams," said Canucks' defenseman Colin Campbell. "Against some teams, you can't give them the blue line. Against Edmonton—especially against Gretzky—you can't give them center ice. With the Oilers' reputation preceding them, teams don't want to get embarrassed."

Game 31, vs. Kings at Los Angeles

For three glorious days, the Oilers left winter behind. They were treated to a midseason vacation at La Costa, a swank California resort for the kind of people who think ice belongs only in a highball and that puck is a Shakespearean character.

Kohos and Victoriavilles were traded in for Ben Hogans and McGregors. The Oilers got a chance to work on their golf games and suntans.

Before the game with the Kings, however, it was one of the LA players who seemed to have had too much sun. Defenseman Mark Hardy, who had eight goals in his career, made a bet that he'd score as many goals as Gretzky in the game at the Fabulous Forum. Hardy did not say how dramatic his goal would be--nor how illegal, if you ask the Oilers.

It took nearly the entire opening period for Edmonton to get started. By then, the Kings had built a 3-0 lead and Sather was wondering what kind of fool would let his team relax on the links for three days in the middle of the season.

Rookie Steve Bozek's 15-footer through a mass of bodies a little over a minute into the game was followed by Dave Taylor's power-play goal and another score by Bozek. But Hughes made it 3-1 at 15:17, then Lumley became only the 11th player in NHL history to score goals in 10 straight games by swinging a backhander at a bouncing puck and sending it over the shoulder of LA goalie Doug Keans.

"I always said I was good at those soft pitch shots," said Lumley, who made his golf lessons pay off.

Then Gretzky got No. 32 on a power play to tie it, only to have Bozek complete his first NHL hat trick on an LA power play at 16:18.

A minute into the third period, Messier converted a perfect pass from Anderson, then Hughes scored his second of the night on a 35-foot drive and the Oilers seemed home free.

Until Hardy made good on his bet.

"He was two feet outside the line," claimed Low, who was watching the critical play from the bench. "It was offsides. We all stopped and hesitated

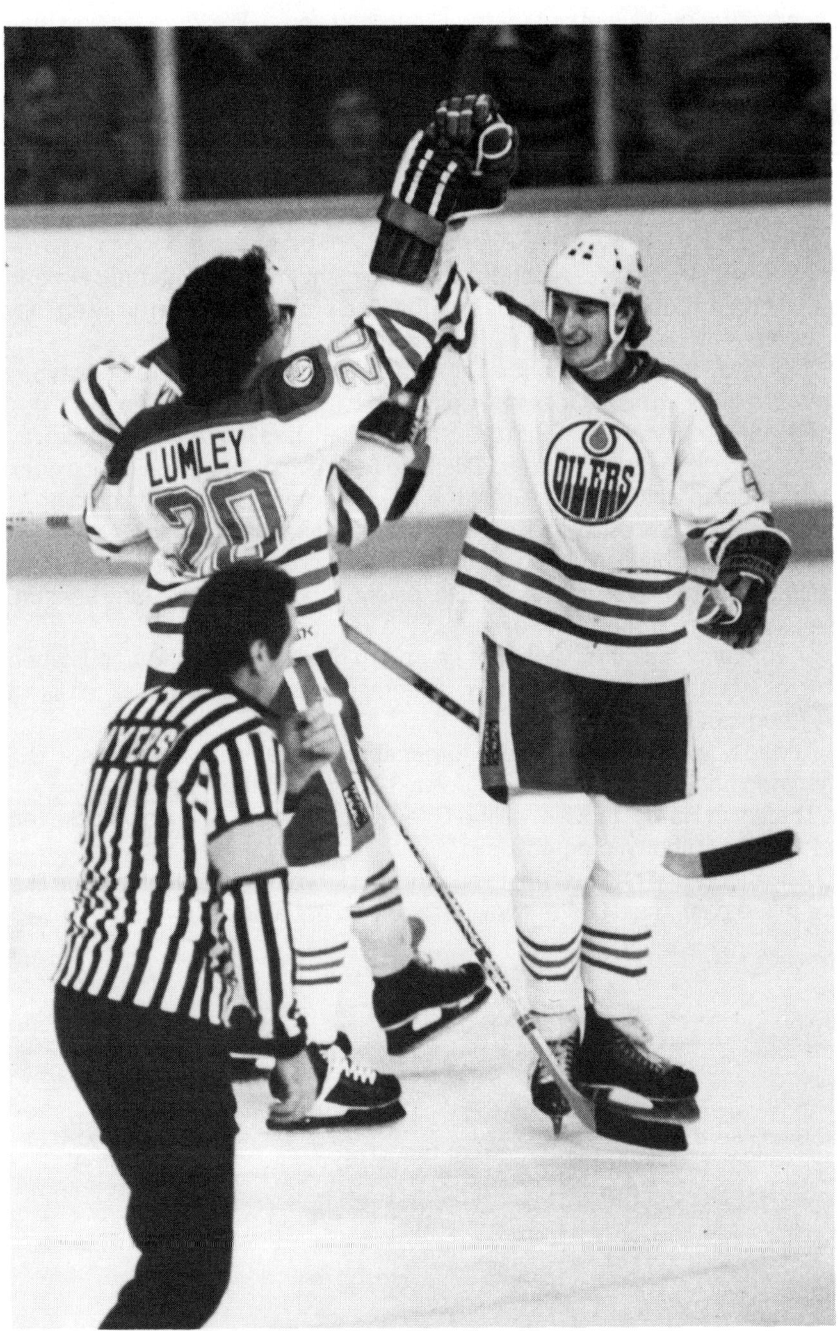

A familiar scene during Lumley's streak.

because the puck went out (of the Edmonton zone). We were waiting for a whistle."

It never came from the linesman. Not that referee Dave Newell was without blame, according to Fuhr, who made only 21 saves in one of his weakest performances to date.

"All I know is somebody hooked the legs out from under me as Hardy was shooting," said Fuhr. "They did it all night. I don't know what Newell was watching."

As for Hardy, he was wearing a great big smile after the game. He had matched The Great Gretzky goal for goal and produced the game-tying tally to boot.

"Not bad," he said. "Not bad at all for a non-scoring defenseman. Maybe I should ask for a raise. Or switch positions."

Gretzky also was upset with the officiating. He had beaten Keans midway through the third period with the Oilers up 5-4. At first, Newell called it a goal, then he decided that the puck hit the post and never went in, according to Gretzky. "You don't see a ref change his mind like that too often."

Sather probably had changed his mind about the value of three days at La Costa. And, thrilled as they were with the short vacation from a long season, the Oilers were wondering how much the vacation had cost them.

"Two days off skates might not seem like much," said Coffey, "but when you're used to the grind every day, it seemed a lot longer. My stick felt like it weighed 1,000 pounds."

Added Lowe, "It took a while to forget about the fairways at La Costa. But we came back strong after being down 3-0. We had them beat."

Thanks to Hardy, though, all the Oilers got was a tie. Still, Lowe believed his team had shown progress.

"The difference between this year and last is we would've lost a game like this in the past," said Lowe. "Now, at least we get a point."

Game 32, vs. Islanders at Edmonton

The champion Islanders stumbled into town at the end of a seven-game road trip in which they'd dropped four and tied one, hardly the calibre of play expected from the best team in the NHL. They were in a nasty mood, seeming to growl rather than speak when confronted with the sad figures of the past two weeks.

They also were in no mood to talk about the red-hot Oilers, who were doing unto others what the Islanders had been doing for two seasons. And they certainly didn't want to hear about Gretzky's record pace and how the Edmonton scoring machine has usurped the title of hockey's best player from Bryan Trottier.

Actually, Gretzky and Trottier both have too much class to be drawn into a shouting match about which one does what better. In fact, they seem to have formed a Mutual Admiration Society.

"He's fun to watch," said Trottier, a seven-year veteran center who has been a dominant player in the NHL right from the start of his rookie season in 1975. "Maybe not so much fun to play against, but he sure does some great things out there."

Trottier is not a man of many words. He is, however, a player of consummate skills with and without the puck. A relentless worker, he enjoys checking, passing and just plain annoying the enemy as much as putting the black disc into the net.

He also carries a burning desire to excel and enjoys being recognized for his achievements, though he claims otherwise. Trots had always been pleased with the positive publicity and accolades thrown his way. He wasn't distraught by the fact that Gretzky was hogging the spotlight—Trots understood that No. 99 had earned that—but he was bothered a bit at being overlooked.

In some ways, Trottier is the kind of all-around player people would like to see Gretzky become. But Trottier, for all his offensive skills—he led the league in scoring in 1978-79 with 134 points—can't match the creativity and sheer scoring power of Gretzky.

What Trots may lack in comparison with Gretzky as an offensive force, he makes up for with intensity and total dedication to stopping opponents. In that way, he's as effective for the Islanders as Wayne is for the Oilers.

"Trottier is a great player," admitted Gretzky. "He never quits coming at you at both ends."

The Oilers entered the game with only one loss in their last 13. They were atop the NHL standings and Gretzky was alone in the points parade. Not Trottier, Mike Bossy or any of their teammates—or counterparts throughout the NHL—was in a position to challenge Gretzky.

Even with the multitudes who were becoming believers in Gretzky above all else, there were some who steadfastly stood in Trottier's corner. Overlooking the fact that Wayne has the puck so often and is doing so much with it that his checking skills (or lack thereof) do not matter much in the Oilers' system, they chose Trottier as the NHL's No. 1 performer.

"I'll take Trottier, even with all the points and records Wayne has," said Harry Neale. "He's been there twice. He's led the Islanders to two Stanley Cups and he's been one of their best players every night. He's more consistent and he's made good things happen for his team.

"When Gretzky does that, he'll prove he's as good as Trottier," added Neale, who would see his team surrender four goals and 18 points to Gretzky in 1981-82. "Nobody can touch Gretzky or what he does with the puck and for scoring. But Trottier does more overall."

"Checking is still a very important part of hockey," added Emile Francis, who runs the St. Louis Blues. "Sure, there were all kinds of crazy scores and Gretzky's responsible for a lot of that. The game has opened up and he's the best there is in that kind of game.

"But Trottier forechecks and backchecks as well as anyone and he's a tougher player. He can do more damage in your zone. He eliminates people. He can make the play and force a guy to give up the puck."

Just as Gretzky and Trottier wouldn't allow themselves to be drawn into comparisons, neither would their coaches take part. Sather has said, when asked about other hockey greats past and present, that he's just happy to have Wayne on his side. Arbour has echoed those sentiments regarding Trottier.

On this night, however, Trottier would come up with one of the most indifferent and ineffective efforts of his career and be shut out. He was no match

Two of hockey's best defensemen—Denis Potvin and Stefan Persson of the Islanders—are virtually defenseless against the onrushing No. 99.

for Gretzky, who had a goal and three assists, including a setup of Lumley, who scored in his 11th straight contest, two shy of Charlie Simmer's league record. The Oilers won 4-3.

New York moved ahead 1-0 only 1½ minutes in, but Gretzky's perfect feed gave Lumley his goal to tie it later in the first period. Lumley fanned on his shot, then got his stick on the puck when it jumped into the air.

Again, the Isles took the lead in the second period when Bob Nystrom beat Fuhr, but Gretzky helped Semenko and Coffey score before John Tonelli knotted it again midway through the period.

A tie seemed assured as both clubs played conservatively in the third session. But, as Sather said so many times during the season, "When you've got Wayne on your side, nothing is certain."

When Gretzky broke free and fired the puck past his old friend, Smith, with only 1:02 left, his celebration seemed a bit more animated, his joy perhaps a tinge deeper than when he scored some of his other 32 goals. It was Smith, after all, who had swatted him across the knee with his goal stick six weeks ago. It was Smith who badmouthed him after the confrontation.

Wayne was asked whether the game-winner was extra special because of those factors.

"It's probably the happiest I've been after scoring a goal," he said. "With a minute left and playing the Islanders, all we wanted to do was make sure Potvin or Bossy or Trottier didn't score on us."

The puck was bouncing along the New York blue line when Gretzky grabbed it, moved around defenseman Denis Potvin and shot.

"I could have gone in further (than 30 feet) but I remembered Smith stopped Lummer when he tried to deke him," said Gretzky, "I was hoping to catch him off-guard."

He didn't as Smith made the save, but the rebound came right to Wayne.

"It went under my arm," Smith reported in describing the ensuing shot. "I made the first save but what can you do? It was about the only good goal they scored."

"At first, I thought I was offside," said Gretzky. "I almost stopped because I thought I heard a whistle."

As if to put the final mark on their encounter, Trottier praised Gretzky, saying, "Wayne made a dynamite play. And he finished it off."

Game 33, vs. Rockies at Colorado

If Dave Lumley looked over to his left and saw a little guy named "Tattoo" skating with him, he wouldn't have batted an eyelash.

"It's like Fantasy Island out there with Wayne," said Lumley, who moved within one game of the modern consecutive game goal-scoring streak of 13, which LA's Simmer set in 1979-80. Lumley scored twice (and added two assists) in a 7-4 romp over the Rockies. "Everybody is so worried about him that he's going to make a fool of them, they don't pay attention to the other guys out there. So I'm just going for the open spaces and he puts it on my stick every time. It's the most fun you can have playing this game."

Gretzky had plenty of fun in Denver, too, scoring once and assisting on two goals. The Oilers set a team record with four goals in 3:39, the four fastest ever scored by Edmonton.

Just 59 seconds into the contest, Gretzky began the onslaught with his 34th goal. Wayne cut from behind the Colorado net and put a backhander into the top corner past goalie Chico Resch. At 2:46, Unger tipped home a pass from Lowe; then Messier scored at 3:25 on a second rebound. That set a team mark for fastest three goals at the start of a period.

When Gretzky set up Coffey for a long slapshot with the Oilers shorthanded 14 seconds later, it was 4-0.

"Their defense stayed in the dressing room the first four minutes," said Lumley. "Resch must look at his Stanley Cup ring (from when he was with the Islanders) and cry, the poor guy."

Gretzky felt no such pity.

"When it was 4-0," he said, "I looked over at Lummer and said, 'Let's fill the net.'"

With the game effectively over, Gretzky and friends decided it was only right to get Lumley a goal. On this night when everything was going right for Edmonton, it wouldn't take long for Lumley to stretch the streak to 12.

At 16:41, the Oilers skated up ice on a 4-on-1 break, with Gretzky leading the charge.

"I knew Lummer was right behind me, so I dropped it to him," said Gretzky. "He knew just what to do with it."

Lumley put a shot over Resch's glove.

He got another goal in the second period as the Oilers made things easy for Billy Harris, who was coaching in place of Sather. Sather had stayed home because of an inner ear infection.

"I'd rather be facing Montreal or Boston," said Harris before the game. "That would take the pressure off if we happen to lose. Everyone expects us to come in here and win."

After three minutes, 39 seconds, Harris had to be glad to be in Denver.

Lumley, meanwhile, was happy just to be in the NHL. He was closing in on one of hockey's most difficult feats to match just a month after he seemed headed for Wichita of the CHL.

"I know how close I was to going to the minors," he admitted. Lumley had scored only seven goals in 1980-81 and was on Sather's hit list at the start of this season. "If Patty (Hughes) doesn't get hurt (strained knee ligaments against the Islanders on November 14) and I don't do well in my first game, I'm gone to Wichita. I hadn't played in so long, I would've been gone, to play myself into shape. I might not have gotten back."

Sather says that Lumley was lucky. Of course, anyone who gets a chance to team with Gretzky is a most fortunate individual.

"I had a ticket for him to Wichita," Sather noted. "At that time, the main reason he was still with us was that he kept working hard even though he wasn't in the lineup."

But then he broke into the lineup and, with Gretzky's aid, here he was on the verge of history.

How much did Gretzky help? In nine of the 12 games, Gretzky assisted on Lumley goals.

"I can't explain it," Lumley said. "When you play with someone as great, as creative and as smart as Wayne, you'll get more scoring opportunities than most players. No one holds the puck better, is more patient for the play to develop, makes a better play or pass. If you get open, he'll find you. But other guys have been on his line and I'm the only one who had this kind of streak."

Sather refused to give Gretzy extra credit. He seemed proud of Lumley's achievement, especially in light of how far Lumley had fallen since a 20-goal, 58-point rookie campaign.

"Wayne helps a lot of players, there's no question about that," said Sather, an Equal Opportunity Employer in that he gives all of his wings a chance to pad their stats skating with Gretzky. "But some guys can't handle the pressure of having to play with him. Lumley has not let either the streak or having to play with Wayne affect his style of play. I feel he's gained a new confidence in his ability that has made him a much better two-way player."

Lumley felt the added ice time, the presence of Gretzky, good fortune and confidence all were key ingredients in the streak.

"I got three or four scoring chances a game and one or two were going in," he explained. "Good shots, bad shots, game after game, one or two went in. Even a penalty shot which I put in. The streak was building before I realized it.

"I hadn't really been thinking about it until the last couple of games. Who would think a guy who made his mark as an aggressive checker would have such a scoring streak? A reporter came up to me before the 10th game of the streak and told me that the record book showed only guys who scored in 10 games in a row. I figured that nine wouldn't mean a thing and it would be great to get the 10th game.

"Knowing that 17,000 people in the building that night were aware of the streak was something that made me want to score so bad," he said. "I didn't want to disappoint the fans.

"When they gave me a two-minute standing ovation after scoring, I had a feeling that can't be described. After scoring in that game, I can honestly say it was the highlight. Everything after that would be gravy."

Lumley even admitted to feeling pangs of guilt because his scoring streak had taken away Gretzky's concentration on his own stats.

"Since my streak started, Wayne's been feeding me instead of trying for his own goals," said Lumley. "I owe the streak to him in many ways, even though he hasn't assisted on all the goals."

Just how much did Lumley feel he owed Gretzky?

"Whatever he wants."

Game 34, vs. Flames at Calgary

It was glorious while it lasted.

Lumley may never get a chance to bask in the spotlight as he did over the past dozen games, but he'll always have the streak to remember and cherish.

It ended in Calgary as the Oilers edged the Flames 5-4. The victory appeared very costly because Fuhr injured his right shoulder with six minutes left in the second period and the Oilers trailing 3-2. The young goalie was run over by Calgary right wing Jamie Hislop, was taken from the ice on a stretcher and had his shoulder popped back into place (ouch!) by the Flames' doctor.

"It's a dislocation," said Sather, who returned to coaching after missing the game in Denver. "He could be out for 10 days, two weeks, six or eight weeks."

"I didn't even see Hislop coming," explained Fuhr. "It was a complete surprise. I landed on the shoulder the wrong way."

This was one game in which Gretzky and his buddies had no chance to try and set up Lumley for the record-tying goal. They were too busy trying to keep pace with an inspired Calgary club.

The Flames opened up a 2-0 lead 8½ minutes in, but Siltanen and Coffey tied it early in the second period. Willi Plett and Mel Bridgman lifted the Flames back into a two-goal margin with just over eight minutes remaining.

Then, as they so often have done this season, the Oilers put together a quick scoring burst to turn it around. Just 30 seconds after Bridgman's breakaway goal against Low, who had replaced Fuhr, Coffey's superb solo rush was stopped by Flames goalie Pat Riggin. Hughes was there to put in the rebound.

A little over two minutes later, Gretzky tied it.

"When I got the puck," said Messier, "I looked up and I knew Gretz was going to be clear. All I had to do was pass to him."

Gretzky sped away, behind the Calgary defense. He faked Riggin and slid the puck home.

"As soon as Riggin stuck his stick out, I knew I was going to deke him," Gretzky said. "I saw his stick slide out and I put the puck under him.

"That was one of the finest plays I've ever seen him make," he added, referring to Messier's pass. "He recognized the situation right away and he didn't hesitate."

The Oilers were not through. With 51 seconds left, Lowe's 40-footer went in off Calgary defenseman Phil Russell.

"I just lobbed the puck at the net," said Lowe. "Then I saw it change direction and the red light was on."

Gretzky was pumped up about the comeback, about the three goals in 7:16.

"Look at a guy like Hughes," he said. "He goes out there grinding, scores to get us close, and it lifts the entire team. That's what we are all about.

"This was a good hockey game for both teams, with a lot of action. It's a good game to win."

It also was the beginning of the most memorable two-week span of Gretzky's life.

Game 35, vs. North Stars at Edmonton

Lumley got back on the right track and Gretzky just kept right on going to form a two-man wrecking crew against the North Stars.

The Oilers allowed Minnesota some false security in the form of a 3-1 lead in the first 5:38 of play. But, by the end of the opening 20 minutes, the Oilers led 5-4, Gretzky had two goals and an assist and Lumley a goal and an assist.

After two periods, Minnesota had forged a 6-6 tie and both Gretzky and Lumley had another assist. Then the Oilers blew it open, with Lumley scoring twice and seting up a tally by Gretzky for a 9-6 triumph.

All told, Gretzky had three goals and four assists and Lumley three and three.

"Wayne thrives on games like this," said Lumley, who didn't make out too badly with his first NHL hat trick and first six-point game. "When there's no hitting, that's his game. I could see his eyes light up."

Gretzky agreed that the lack of contact and checking in the game was to his advantage.

"When you get that much room, you're bound to be able to make the plays," he said. "The North Stars are a pretty good skating and shooting team. But I think they realize they made a mistake trying to outgun us."

On his first goal, Gretzky faked out Minnesota's Ron Meighan, who could only flail with his stick as Wayne went by. Then Gretzky got by goalie Gilles Meloche, who had wandered too far out of the net, and put home his 36th goal.

His second goal came from a scramble in front of Meloche. Gretzky was the only one to spot the puck in a jumble of bodies and he poked it in.

Gretzky, ever graceful, being checked by North Stars defenseman Gordie Roberts.

Gretzky, a beaten defenseman, an unprotected goaltender . . . seconds later, one of Gretzky's 92 goals.

"I'm getting more goals than ever like that, on pileups and scrambles," he noted.

He completed the hat trick with a 25-foot shot that went under Meloche's arm.

Neither coach was especially impressed by the brand of hockey they'd just witnessed.

"You could see it coming right off the bat," said Sather. "Our team was buzzing and they got a few early goals. You knew it wouldn't stop there. At least we had Wayne Gretzky."

"Of all the teams to get into a shootout with, this is the worst," said North Stars coach Glen Sonmor. "We haven't been getting goals lately and now, we finally get some and we want to get in a shooting derby.

"We've got a lot of selfish hockey players who think the way to play this game is to fish for the puck continually. Their thinking is, 'If I come up with the puck, I'd get a few points.' And they aren't all forwards either.

"They see what Gretzky can do and they all think they'll try to do it. But they don't understand how great he is and that there's no one around who can do what he does.

"If it's one or two players, it's pretty easy to do something about it. But when the disease affects the whole team, it's pretty tough.

"We're apparently unwilling to pay the price it takes to battle our way through these things," added Sonmor, who kept repeating his disbelief that his players would attempt to stage a shootout against the most potent attack in hockey. "If you continually try to come up with the puck and don't run into anybody, you're going to get beaten.

"The easy way to play this game is to poke the puck. You never get hit with a stick on the side of the head and never get an elbow in the mouth when you do that. It's nice and easy."

The Oilers wouldn't mind a full season of what Sonmor termed "scoring derbies."

"They jumped into an early lead and we had to open it up and they thought, 'Fine, we'll play a wide open game,'" said Lumley. "Anybody who comes into our building and wants to do that is just going to get blown out."

Game 36, vs. Flames at Edmonton

Glen Sather made his mark as an NHL player with his mouth and his fists. In his nine pro seasons with six different clubs, Sather was an instigator, a belligerent type who badgered opponents and referees.

He scored all of 80 goals and 193 points in those nine seasons, about the kind of numbers being projected for Gretzky this year.

As a coach, however, Sather is a lot tamer. Every once in a while, though, he loses control and the old "Slats" surfaces.

At home, as the Oilers fell to the Flames 7-5, that's precisely what happened. At the end of the game, in which the Oilers fell apart in the third period, Sather was fuming. He let loose with enough steam to power any oil rig in Alberta.

"I can understand why a guy like (Philadelphia's Paul) Holmgren can punch a referee if the officials are as incompetent as the ones we saw tonight," said Sather. He was referring to an incident in which Holmgren, in his attempts to get at Pittsburgh's Paul Baxter, slugged ref Andy Van Hellemond. "It wasn't a game against Calgary. It was a game against Myers, Bozak and Christison.

"Why is it we get the same three guys two nights in a row? Is the league trying to save money by not bringing anybody else in? They can fine me for saying this but I won't pay it."

Sather was most annoyed by a game misconduct penalty handed to Lowe in the first period, referee Bob Myers' call of a Calgary goal by Ken Houston and linesman Ryan Bozak's disallowing of an Oilers' score.

"I'm going to keep yelling and they'll have to have an inquiry," he said,

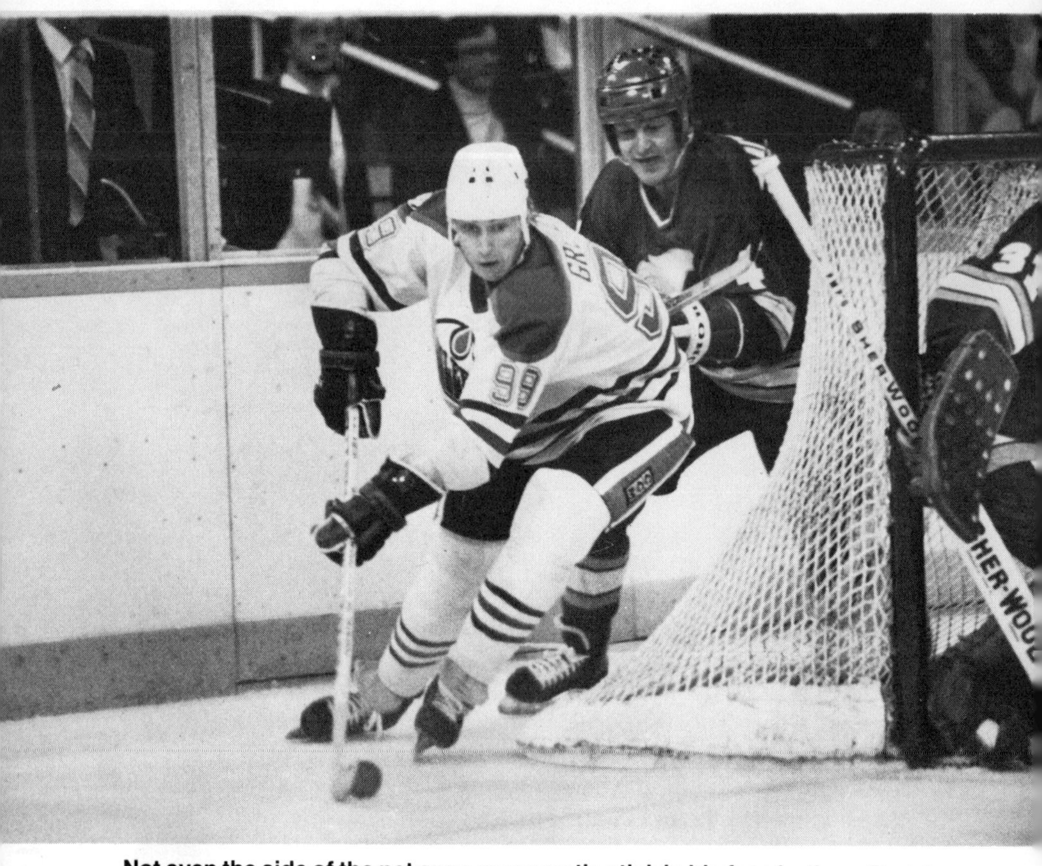

Not even the side of the net or an opponent's stick in his face bothers Gretzky.

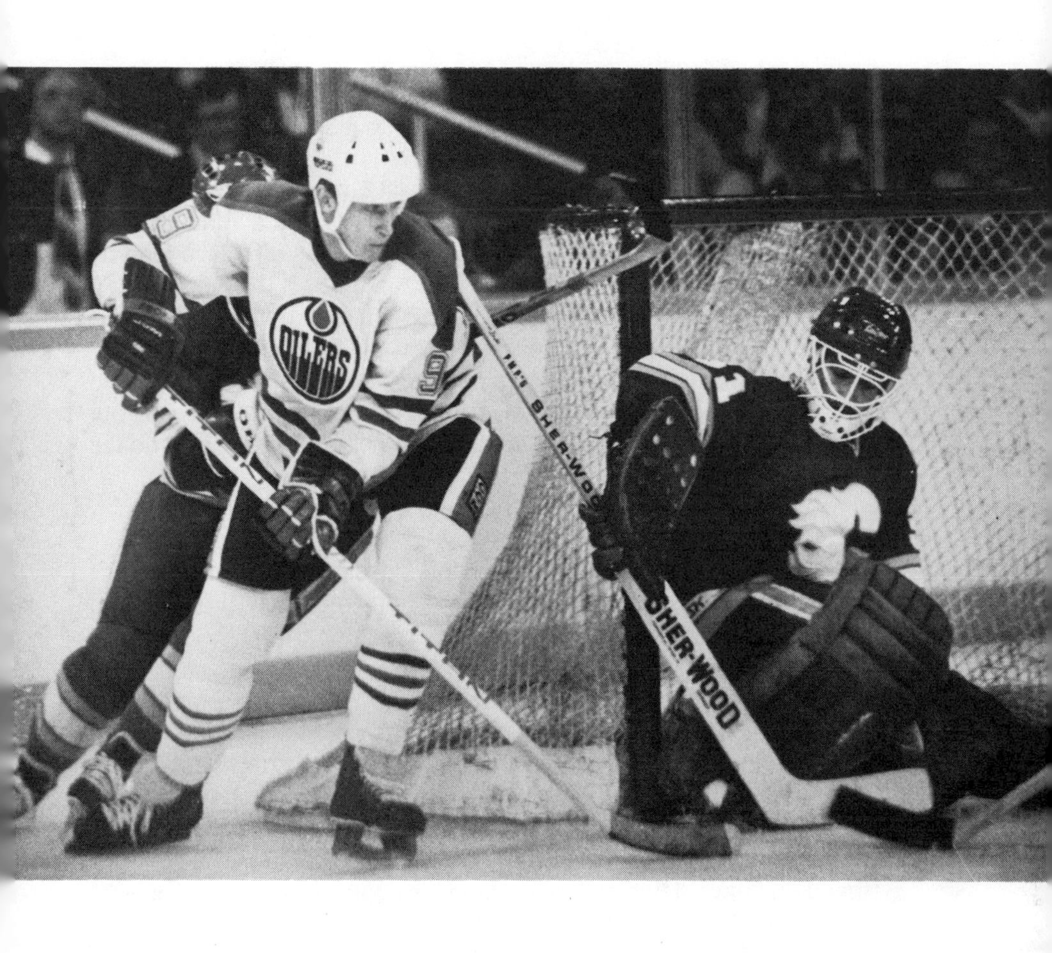
OILERS
SHER-WOOD
SHER-WOOD

"That's what I want. I'm going to have film to prove my point. Instead of isolating on our players with a camera, I told them to just watch Myers for the last two periods."

Gretzky scored twice in the second period to lift Edmonton into a 4-3 lead. His first goal, 11 seconds into a power play, came on a masterful tip-in of Siltanen's slapshot from the point. The second one was off a nice feed by Callighen and gave Gretzky 40 goals.

He also fed Lee Fogolin for a shot from the slot with 1:11 left to pull the Oilers within 6-5, but Lanny McDonald clinched it with an empty-netter.

In between Gretzky's goals, Anderson's pass from the corner went into the Calgary net off Messier's skate. Myers immediately signaled a goal, but Bozak overruled it, saying Messier intentionally kicked the puck past goalie Rejean Lemelin.

"I went to stop so I didn't run into the net," explained Messier, "and the puck hit my foot."

As if that call—television replays indicated Messier was correct—wasn't enough to insense Sather and the Oilers, Houston's tally provided the incentive for the coach's tirade.

"Both teams head to the blue line for a faceoff and he (Myers) carried the puck to center ice and says, 'Goal,'" Sather shouted. "The Flames didn't even think it was good. They were as shocked as we were."

Mel Bridgman's game-winner was the flukiest goal of the night. Bridgman, standing in Gretzky territory behind the enemy net, sent a pass out that hit the skate of Fogolin and squirted past Moog, who had been recalled earlier in the week when Fuhr was hurt.

Sather didn't have anything to say about his goalie, who stopped only 21 of 28 shots. He didn't need to say much: Moog soon returned to the minor leagues, where he remained the rest of the season.

Game 37, vs. Canucks at Edmonton

The big news for the Oilers was the return of Fuhr, who sparkled while making 33 saves in a 6-1 romp. The big news for Gretzky was a goal and three assists, pushing his total for 37 games to 93 points and, combined with his last 43 contests of the previous season, gave him an even 200 points in his last 80 games, the equivalent of one full schedule.

"That's not the way they count them," he said.

Harry Neale was impressed with Fuhr's performance, especially in the second period, when he stopped all 16 shots which came his way.

"Young Fuhr looked like Old Fuhr," said Neale. "We had a pretty good period and it's discouraging when you outshoot a team and they have a bad period and you get zip."

Late in the first period, Gretzky set up Kurri to put the Oilers on top to stay. Kurri planted himself deep in the slot and Gretzky, naturally, found him.

In the third period, Semenko, causing all kinds of havoc in front of the Vancouver net on a power play, knocked in Gretzky's pass and Lumley got his 20th goal, tying his career high, when Gretzky sprung him on a Vancouver power play.

Lumley returned the favor with 1:14 left, feeding Wayne in front of Canucks goalie Glen Hanlon. Gretzky put in a short shot for No. 41.

"Not a bad night," Lumley said. "I think we're ready to roll."

Game 38, vs. Kings at Edmonton

Lumley was right. The Oilers rolled over Los Angeles, which had been humiliated 11-4 on its last trip to Edmonton. This time it was 10-3 and Gretzky duplicated his four-goal game in the previous home outing with the Kings.

The four goals gave Gretzky 13 in his last eight games and at least one goal in each of the eight. He was, as Anderson noted, "on fire."

Not only did the Oilers smash the Kings, but LA rolled over like a dead fish in the third period, when Edmonton scored five times against abandoned goalie Mario Lessard.

"When you see guys like Dionne and other veterans giving up," said Lowe, "the younger players on their team must wonder what's going on."

Gretzky's third and fourth goals both came with Edmonton shorthanded. He had connected twice in the first period as the Oilers moved ahead 3-0, then rookie Steve Bozek scored a pair to put the Kings back in contention. No matter.

With Semenko in the box, Gretzky picked up a loose puck at center ice, beat Jay Wells with one of the patented "See You Later, Sucker" moves, then slid the puck under Lessard as the goalie tried to knock it off Gretzky's stick.

Kurri, Anderson and Ken Berry, with his first NHL goal, followed, then Gretzky connected once more on a Kings' power play. This time, he broke free of the defense and beat Lessard on a breakaway with a clean wrist shot.

With an assist on a goal by Hicks, Gretzky totaled five points, pushing him over the 100-point mark. If it wasn't clear by now that the heretofore unmentioned 200-point mountain was about to be scaled, Gretzky's stats for the first 38 games put it sharply into focus.

"Wayne is kind of the cream that makes this team go," Sather understated. "Everybody talks about his ability but he works hard, as hard as anybody else. I'll never stop watching him and enjoying him play."

Bruce MacGregor, the Oilers' assistant GM, watched Gretzky's sensational show and recognized exactly what was going on and why.

"Hockey is a game of where people should be and where people are going to be," he said. "Gretz anticipates those things so well he is two or three steps ahead of everybody.

"I'll go on the ice with him and it's amazing to see some of the things he does. He gives you a lot of quick moves with the puck and then he's gone.

"For a hockey player, the stick has to be part of your body. It's really an extension of your body. You have to have that feel for it. Wayne has it. You seldom see him look at the puck."

You hardly ever notice him surveying the positioning of the players on the ice, either. But he knows where everyone is and, more important, he knows where everyone is headed.

And, after another demolition of the Kings, Wayne knew where he was headed. The 50-goal galaxy was next and his rocket boosters were ready to fire.

On his way to 50, Gretzky is slowed down . . . temporarily.

Game 39, vs. Flyers at Edmonton

"I don't ever go into a game thinking I'll get five goals, but I never go in thinking I can't."

Gretzky was in the process of proving he can do practically anything on the ice. Once before in his 2½ seasons of NHL duty, he had managed five goals in one night— against St. Louis in February 1981. He needed that many to reach 50 goals after his four-goal spree against the Kings three nights earlier.

Only two men had ever collected 50 goals in the first 50 games of a season. Maurice Richard, "The Rocket," who was the most fearsome scorer of his day, did it in a 50-game season back in 1944-45. Mike Bossy of the Islanders equaled that achievement in the last two minutes of the 50th game of last season.

Now, Gretzky was on the verge of shattering the 50-in-50 mark to pieces. He even spoke of the unthinkable: 50 in 40.

"Fifty goals in 50 games would be an honor," he said. "It would put me in there with great players like Richard and Bossy. But 50 in 40 . . . well, we've got only two games left. I'd like to do it but Philadelphia and Vancouver are two good defensive teams."

Obviously, Gretzky hadn't seen the 1981-82 version of the Broad Street Bullies. The Flyers, hurting for experienced, mobile defenseman and also weak on the wings and unsteady with a three-man goaltending rotation which was causing confusion and low confidence among the goalies, had been mauled 11-2 in Montreal earlier in the season. In one stretch, beginning with that humiliation by the Canadiens, they gave up 42 goals in six games.

99

On the way to 50 goals, Gretzky eludes Philly's Bill Barber.

Philly also had been embarrassed by the lowly Washington Capitals 10-4 and had given up 14 goals in the last three contests entering this game. The Flyers were exactly the type of opponent Gretzky could exploit.

But five goals in a game? It had only been done 17 times since 1930 prior to this season.

Still, reaching 50 at home in the 39th game of the season would be a nice New Year's present for himself and the Edmonton fans. So, as Wayne Gretzky left his home on the afternoon of December 30, he turned to Lowe and said he thought he "could do it tonight."

With the Flyers on top 1-0, Gretzky began his assault. Philly's Brian Propp was in the penalty box when Coffey fed Wayne down the boards. The power play was nearly over and Gretzky had spent the length of it trying to direct an Oiler score.

As the puck arrived from Coffey, Gretzky cut to the slot and put it between the pads of goalie Pete Peeters. That was No. 46.

"After Wayne got the first goal, Ron Low looked at me and said, 'I bet you he'll do it tonight,'" Sather recalled.

Just 2:25 later, he was back on Peeters' doorstep. Lumley and Semenko drew the Flyer defensemen to the slot area and Gretzky skated in behind to whip a shot from the netminder's left which caromed in off the far goal post. No. 47.

Gretzky went back to playmaking to help set up Coffey's power-play goal and the period ended with Edmonton ahead 3-1.

Reggie Leach got the Flyers back within 3-2 at 3:44 of the middle period, but Gretzky didn't dawdle. He waited all of 10 seconds before making it 4-1.

Lumley anticipated a breakout pass by Bobby Clarke and stole it. He hit Gretzky in full flight and Wayne put the puck over Peeters' shoulder. No. 48.

By now, the fans were in a frenzy, fully realizing that Gretzky had 36 minutes in which he needed two goals.

"He was playing like a man obsessed," said Clarke. "Everytime he gets a chance, he scores. It's worse than Orr. At least he started in his own end and you could brace yourself in some kind of a defense to stop it. Gretzky materializes out of nowhere.

"You think he's out of the play and then he's there. And it's in the net. They say he just has a knack . . . that the puck follows him around. But it happens too often for it to be just that. He's got to know. Every damn time, he's got to know."

By now, Gretzky most assuredly knew 50 goals were attainable on this night. But first he needed the 49th and he was blanked the rest of the second period.

"I wasn't thinking I had only 20 minutes to score twice," he claimed. "It was still a close game (5-3 Edmonton). I knew we'd need more goals."

Five minutes into the third period, Gretzky screwed defenseman Bob Hoffmeyer into the ice with one of his spectacular moves, the kind he makes about every shift or so. Then he blasted a shot over Peeters' shoulder. No. 49.

The 17,490 fans in the Coliseum were making about as much noise as the building could stand. Whenever Gretzky came back on the ice, which was often, the noise level somehow intensified. One writer turned to a colleague next to him and, at the top of his lungs, asked the other writer a question. Then he repeated it. And again he repeated it. The other writer heard nothing.

The Flyers may not be the most talented group of hockey players anymore, but they are gritty. And, in the face of a crowd gone bonkers, they rallied.

Peeters twice stopped Gretzky on clear shots; then Paul Holmgren, who was back in action after serving a seven-game suspension for pushing a referee, and Fred Arthur beat Fuhr within 17 seconds to make it 6-5.

With the minutes ticking away, Edmonton failed on a power play, then was forced to skate shorthanded for two minutes when Kurri's stick was found to have an illegal curve. The score remained 6-5 and anticipation of Peeters being lifted for an extra attacker grew.

With 1:14 to go, out came Peeters. Almost immediately, as if destiny was pushing the puck to him, Gretzky got a hold of it behind the red line and slid a shot towards the gaping net.

It went wide and the Oilers were called for icing.

Once more, Gretzky got control and, as he skated to the Philadelphia blue line, Flyers center Ken Linseman caught up and knocked the puck away. The Flyers began a final attack at Fuhr.

A long shot rebounded off Fuhr's stick to Anderson, who didn't hesitate. He sent the puck to center ice. He didn't look. He didn't have to. He knew—everyone knew—who would be there.

Gretzky accepted the pass and went one-on-one against Philly's Bill Barber. Gretzky cut to the middle as Barber lunged to swipe at the puck. At the same time, Wayne shot. There were three seconds on the clock when the puck glided into the open net.

No. 50.

For once, Gretzky seemed overwhelmed by what he had done. Hours earlier, he'd admitted to the feeling he might get to 50 on this night. After he had done so, Gretzky was having trouble believing it.

"It's a great feeling but it doesn't compare to beating Montreal in the playoffs last year," he said. "It's great to get individual records like this, especially when the team wins. And I'm in with people like Maurice Richard and Mike Bossy. It's a thrill."

Gretzky later admitted that this was probably his best game in the NHL. But Sather disagreed, warning that, "We haven't seen his best yet."

Indeed, Clarke offered the opinion that Gretzky was making the impossible routine.

"It's obscene," said Clarke. "There are going to be records broken, but not the way he's doing it. You hear, well, the game has changed, it's more wide open since expansion. Then why hasn't anyone else done what Gretzky and Orr have done. Because they're that much better than the rest of us.

"You hear Gretzky's not that great a skater. Hell, I'll bet there aren't more than a handful of players in the league who are faster than he is.

"And the shot. It's hard and anyone who says it isn't is kidding themselves. Again, there may be only a few guys around today who shoot harder. And, obviously, his timing and vision are superior to the rest of us.

"But even so, it's unbelievable what he's doing. You know teams are trying to devise strategies against him. He sees a checking line every game and he annihilates them."

As Gretzky prepared to leave the arena, he could still hear the chants of "GRETZKY, GRETZKY" which emanated from the stands after he scored No. 49 and pursued 50.

"You know," he said, "that was some kind of feeling, knowing that the last time the people did that was for Guy (Lafleur) in the Canada Cup. Woo, that's nice."

While Gretzky appeared unable to express the significance of his accomplishment, others were quite willing to extol the virtues of a youngster who was doing things at 20 which the best players in hockey history wouldn't have dreamed of at the same age.

"It's a privilege to be on the same ice with him," said Clarke. "Like any great player—Orr, Howe, Beliveau—he is something else.

"And he's 20 years old. Twenty years old!!

"Obviously, there were things we could have done better against him, but nobody will ever shut him down. You think you have him and he spins away almost every time. This is crazy, absolutely crazy."

"Any superlatives I might suggest would be inadequate after a performance like that," said Flyers coach Pat Quinn. "I thought to myself today, 'Well, at least I won't have to worry about him getting 50 against us.' If anybody told me before the game that he'd get five goals against us tonight, I'd have lost a lot of money betting against it."

Game 40, Canucks at Vancouver

It was New Year's Eve and the Oilers, who'd done their celebrating the night before after Gretzky's spree to 50, were in no mood to spend the holiday away from home. They also were in no mood to play hockey.

They didn't, falling 3-1 to the Canucks and not scoring until less than four minutes remained, when Anderson connected. Gretzky was invisible.

"We anticipated a natural letdown," said Sather. "You could sense that tonight might not be a good game for us. Too much happened in too short a time."

Added Anderson: There wasn't much of a chance "for us to regroup for this game. We weren't ready but there was an obvious reason why."

Letdown City.

Game 41, vs. Bruins at Edmonton

The post-50 goals blahs continued as the Oilers blew a 4-1 lead in the final 6:35 and allowed the Bruins to tie them 4-4.

Whenever the Oilers and Bruins meet, the pre and post-game talk centers around Gretzky and his Boston shadow, Steve Kasper. Once again on this night, Kasper did a superb job following Wayne around the ice, barely giving Gretzky room to breathe, and neutralizing him whenever Gretzky did get involved in the action.

Wayne scored a power-play goal with Kasper seated on the bench in the second period to lift the Oilers into a 1-0 margin. It was only the second goal against Boston for Gretzky in nine meetings since the Oilers joined the NHL. Neither of those goals came while Kasper was checking him.

The tally, his 51st of the season, came after Messier made a terrific play to get off a shot at Boston goalie Marco Baron. Messier controlled the rebound the flipped it to the front of the net for Gretzky, who was alone in front with a gaping cage staring at him.

The other point for Gretzky was the result of a bad line change by the Bruins which left Kasper and his linemates too far up ice as Edmonton broke towards Baron with a 2-on-1.

"When Gretzky's one of the two, it's fatal," said Kasper. "You don't have a chance."

Kasper would not allow Wayne another good scoring chance after No. 99 set up Kurri on the 2-on-1 to make it 3-1. Anderson brought the Oilers' edge to 4-1 midway through the third period, but then Boston took command,

Thank God for long arms.

thanks to Brad Park and his aluminum-shafted stick.

Park rifled two blasts from the past—he used to have one of the hardest and most accurate slapshots in hockey—into the Edmonton net as a stunned Fuhr failed to move. The first Park goal, at 13:25 of the final period, came with Gretzky in, of all places, the penalty box, and it started the Bruin comeback.

Less than two minutes later, it was Park once more; then Ray Bourque tied it with 1:45 to go as his slapper from the point hit Hicks on the back of the leg and flew behind Fuhr.

"One day I started to shoot around with the aluminum stick and it seemed to have that old zip on it," said Park, once the second best defenseman in hockey, behind only a guy named Orr. "I was shooting it like I used to seven or eight years ago."

The spotlight deservedly belonged to Park after his standout performance, but he gladly spoke of other things. Park knows a little bit about being compared with the greats of the game, having been a star in New York while Orr was holding court in Boston. He knows what it's like to toil in someone's shadow, just as Gretzky was learning how long and effective a shadow Kasper casts.

"The thing about a superstar is that the more his reputation grows, the better he becomes," said Park. "The more people watch him and play differently, just because he's on the ice, the more he's going to be able to do. You see that now. People are worried as soon as he climbs over the boards."

Bruins coach Gerry Cheevers was plenty concerned about Gretzky prior to the game. He tried not to let on but it was useless.

"I'm trying to stay away from talking about Gretzky," Cheevers explained. "But we will talk about him, of course. It's just that you can't put all your effort into stopping one guy because the Edmonton players are too good.

"The Oilers—or whatever their name is—are a legitimate Stanley Cup contender. A co-favorite.

"I'm looking forward to this game more than a game in Montreal. This is the toughest challenge of the (seven-game) trip.

"As for Gretzky, listen. If I have to play Kasper against him for 60 minutes, I will."

That possibility seemed to be approaching as Sather continued to double or even triple-shift Gretzky and shuffle his personnel around.

"The main idea of what we're doing with Gretzky is to get him away from the people putting a specific line against him.

"When we're moving him around, we not only get him extra ice time, we also get people worrying about what we're doing with Gretzky instead of worrying about playing the game."

Added assistant coach Harris: "Wayne has an extra minute of on-ice endurance that other players don't have. It gives us an opportunity to make the most of that as well."

"I put him on the ice with two different wings and they all get excited about having him at center and they start playing better," continued Sather. "Then I return him to two other wings and they're so glad to have him back, they play terrific.

"It's like having a piece of gold and taking it from one pawn shop to another to find the best deal."

Only, when Sather gets to the Boston Bruins' pawn shop, there's no deal awaiting him.

"I guess it's fair to say you judge Gretzky's play by what numbers he puts on the scoreboard," said Bruins captain Wayne Cashman. "With Stevie, you don't do that at all. You don't judge Stevie's performance by the score sheet because he's the guy keeping it clean.

"Gretzky doesn't dominate us because Stevie dominates him."

Game 42
vs. Rockies at Edmonton

For the fifth time in as many meetings, the Oilers rocked the Colorado net with at least 40 shots. Gretzky had 11 of the 41 missiles sent the way of Rockies goalie Phil Myre, and he scored on two of them in a 5-3 victory.

"They checked us well in the first period and, all of a sudden, it was 3-1," said Gretzky, who, like most of his teammates, had warmed up for the game with a ping-pong tournament. "Luckily, Grant took charge, gave us a boost and kept us going."

The Rockies surrounded Gretzky's 52nd goal with three of their own as the Edmonton defense made like Swiss cheese. Wayne's tally, however, was the most artistic of those scored in the opening 20 minutes.

"That was one of the best individual efforts you'll ever see on a goal," said Harris. What Harris and the sellout crowd had seen was Gretzky complete a superb solo rush by faking defenseman Rob Ramage and Myre, then depositing the puck home.

During the break, Sather laced into his team for not being ready and, when the second period began, the Oilers were spitting fire. Yet it took more than 14 minutes to penetrate the Rockies' net, with Gretzky setting up Messier on a power play.

Wayne had wheeled in center ice to reorganize the power play when he spotted Messier and led him perfectly for a breakaway. Messier, who was developing into one of the most deadly shooters in hockey, converted.

A couple of minutes later, Berry scored his second NHL goal to tie it. The final period belonged to Gretzky and Company.

On the game-winner, Gretzky set up camp behind the Colorado net and threaded a pinpoint pass to Anderson for a five-footer. Wayne then clinched matters with a rising slapshot from 30 feet on his last shot of the game.

"On Anderson's goal, he faked me to the side and passed it while he was still behind the net," said Myre. "I didn't move to the post quick enough. He froze me. I don't know if it's a set play or not. But that's the danger of his being back there. He's so unpredictable and he always seems to find the right move.

"On his last goal, he had a couple of inches to shoot at. He hit it."

Sather wasn't pleased with the difficulty his club had against the doormat Rockies. He wondered if playing ping-pong "was any way to prepare for playing hockey."

Harris thought the Oilers proved something.

"Good teams win a lot of games when they don't play well," he reported. "We're capable of playing a lot better than that and we still got two points."

Game 43, vs. Flames at Edmonton

So often, sports is dominated by contrasts. These two games provided a stark one.

At home, the Oilers did everything right and were inspired by the surprising return to the lineup of Hughes, who went out and scored two goals in a 7-2 walk.

The next night, in the Calgary Stampede Corral, the Flames burned Edmonton 5-1 as Gretzky went scoreless for the sixth time all season.

In the Edmonton game, though Gretzky registered his fifth five-point game of the year—a goal and four assists—the night belonged to Hughes. On December 23 against Vancouver, the right wing had injured his tailbone. Hughes was headed for his best season at that point, with 15 goals in 36 games.

"I came to the rink early to shower but not to play," he said. "Glen asked me if I wanted to skate in the warmup. I said fine.

"Then he said I looked all right and asked me if I'd mind suiting up and killing some penalties. I said fine.

"We took a penalty early (at 1:09) and I got into the game in a hurry. I felt great just being out there again."

Hughes scored twice in the third period on assists by Gretzky. On his first goal, Hughes took a pass from Gretzky and wristed the puck past Calgary goalie Pat Riggin in the same motion. On the second, a three-way passing sequence from Gretzky to Berry to Hughes, all in a couple of seconds, gave Hughes the open side to shoot at.

Gretzky, sporting a new look thanks to a haircut, also assisted on Messier's 28th goal by passing the puck to the winger from behind the Calgary net. His other assist set up Lumley for a quick shot which Riggin never reacted to.

Gretzky's goal, which made it 2-0, was one of the least creative he would score all season. Kurri sent a pass off the boards while the Oilers were shorthanded and Gretzky broke free with the puck. As he skated in on Riggin, the puck decided to go its own way. Still, it trickled into the net.

"They all count," Gretzky said with a smile.

Game 44, vs. Flames at Calgary

A rough first period, during which the Flames seemed intent on proving they were unaffected by the previous night's massacre, and an outburst of goals in the second period lifted Calgary to the victory in the rematch.

"We had no intensity and we were out of it after the first period," said Sather.

"We were humiliated last night and we had to set things straight," retorted Flames defenseman Paul Reinhart.

The opening-period brawl saw Semenko leave the bench to get in his licks. He was thrown out and the Oilers sagged.

Reinhart had three assists and Mel Bridgman added two goals and an assist for the Flames. Gretzky was quiet all night but even Sather admitted he was entitled.

In fact, Gretzky wasn't all that surprised about the loss.

"I think we have been so successful that we got to the point where we started to believe all we had to do was throw our sticks on the ice to win. At the same time that was happening, we became a kind of trophy for other teams. To beat us was special, something to brag about all season."

Game 45, vs. Capitals at Washington

The Washington Capitals have never made the playoffs. They've called last place home for eight seasons.

But even the worst has a chance against the best for, as the time-worn adage goes, "The game starts off even. It's 0-0 when they first drop the puck."

When the Caps left the ice against the Oilers at the Capital Centre, it was 6-6. A point in the standings for both clubs but, for the struggling Caps, a moral victory at the least.

Gretzky and friends began the game with a flurry, making it look like a mismatch, as one might have expected. The Oilers took command 4-2 after one period as Gretzky pumped in Goal No. 55 (less than two minutes in) and set up a pair by Kurri.

Then the Caps stormed back, tying it 5-5 after two periods and, trailing 6-5 after Hunter scored early in the final session, dramatically tying it on Dennis Maruk's 31st goal only 10 seconds from the final buzzer.

Maruk beat Gretzky on a faceoff, sending the puck to Bengt Gustafsson, who quickly returned it to Maruk for the dramatic shot.

"When you're winning 6-5 and finish like that," said Gretzky, "it's just awful. I lost the draw and the next thing I know, it's in the net. It was nobody's fault but mine.

"It's not so bad when you lose the faceoff but when your man scores, it is. Everybody makes mistakes but when you make a mistake like that, it hurts the hockey team. It shouldn't have happened."

On the other side, it was one of the finest moments in Caps' history—with a history that reads like a bad dream, there aren't too many special memories—but it was witnessed by only 3,284 fans. A massive snowstorm had ruined the night for the Capitals, who struggled all season at the gate and were hopeful of a sellout to wipe out some red ink. Instead, they got a lot of white stuff.

But they also got a point, though few of the Caps were ready to claim their game plan for neutralizing Gretzky had worked.

"We did pretty well against him after the first period," said Caps coach Bryan Murray. "I guess you feel good when he doesn't score on you in the last two periods."

Two seasons ago, the Caps were victimized for seven assists by Gretzky, tying an NHL mark for one game. Ever since, they'd been relatively successful against him, holding Wayne scoreless in two of the four 1980-81 meetings: Gretzky struck for two goals and four assists in the other two contests.

This was Washington's first look at the 1982 version of the wonder scorer. They knew what to look for and, after the opening 9:43, they figured out how to cope.

"You have to stay close to him, not right up against him, but close to him, close enough to keep him from passing the puck," said Gustafsson, a decent checking forward from Sweden who drew a portion of the "contain Gretzky" assignment. "As soon as they get the puck, you have to pick him up. There's no other way. You don't worry about him making you look bad, either."

Gustafsson did not use entirely legal means to control Gretzky. Several times he hooked the Oilers' star and Gretzky retaliated twice by slashing at Gustafsson. Referee Kerry Fraser didn't see fit to call any penalties, however, and Gretzky didn't see any reason to bitch afterward.

"I get it all the time and it doesn't really bother me," he said. "Give him credit for working hard and doing his job."

Caps assistant coach Yvon Labre figured that Gretzky makes everybody look bad at one time or another.

"He's like a computer out there," said Labre. "He analyzes everything and then gets himself open. He can adjust to anything and he'll do so almost immediately. You check him one way and he'll go another. Stop him and he'll feed his wingers.

"There are things he does that other players are able to do maybe once. He'll do them every night."

Gretzky did them in the first 10 minutes. The rest of the night was a bummer. Even worse for the Oilers, after they tied the lowly Capitals, they had to trudge through a blizzard.

Game 46, vs. Flyers at Philadelphia

If there was one team which would enter every game against the Oilers with the proper respect for Mr. Gretzky, it was the Flyers.

Even though Edmonton was coming off two subpar efforts, the Flyers weren't about to overlook what the Oilers (and especially Gretzky) are capable of doing. All they had to do—and all most of them were doing—for a refresher was look back two weeks to Wayne's enchanted evening at the Flyers' expense.

"With Gretzky, they could win it all," said Bobby Clarke. "They've got some good kids, like Lowe and Coffey on defense and the kid in goal (Fuhr) apparently is outstanding. And, with a player like Gretzky, they could just blow by everybody. They could win the whole thing.

"This year, with Mark Messier and Glenn Anderson improving so much, the Oilers have two really good players to play with him. But they still spread him around and just look what he does with the other players. Look at what he did last year, when the team wasn't nearly as good.

"They jump on top of everyone so fast. What good is a checking line when you're down 3-0? You try to open it up and you play right into their hands."

Peeters, the goalie at the wrong end when Gretzky surged to 50, mentioned that the one thing Wayne didn't do that night was hurt Philly from behind the net.

"He was too busy shooting, I guess," said Peeters, who was asked what can be done to nullify Gretzky's skills from in back of the cage. "Well, you keep your stick out past the post and that way maybe you can block a pass or two. And you wish you had a periscope so you could see what he was doing without turning around."

Flyers coach Pat Quinn surely had devised some outrageous new technique to neutralize Gretzky—or at least keep him from getting more than a goal or two.

"We watched him on tape and tried to figure out what he'd done and how," said Quinn. "If we play them in the (Stanley Cup) finals or if we faced them eight times like the teams in that division, we'd have to try something. But with only three games against them, we don't have time to put in anything without screwing up other things."

It was the Oilers who screwed up in Philly. The Flyers bolted to a 3-0 margin after 20 minutes, outshooting Edmonton 14-5, then upped it to 7-0 in the second.

With the score 8-1 and 2:48 left, Gretzky got his 56th goal on a 15-footer right after winger Curt Brackenbury screened Peeters.

"It's been coming for 10 days," Sather said after the 8-2 pasting. "We've been ignoring what we were doing to win and we've been sloppy. This was the result of it."

Another result of the lopsided defeat was the calling of a team meeting.

"When something like this happens," said Low, who faced 43 shots and didn't exactly distinguish himself with his play, "the best thing to do is sit down and air a few views. One thing about an 8-2 loss: it has a habit of making meetings such as these happen right away."

For Gretzky, the 56th goal was a professional career high. That rang hollow for him.

"We've been in a lot of games this year where we did that to the other team," he said of the rout. "It doesn't feel very good to be on the wrong side."

Harris, the assistant coach, knew best why it had happened.

"I guess they owed us one," he said. "They sure paid us back."

Game 47, vs. Maple Leafs at Toronto

If the team meeting had any positive affects, it wasn't apparent in Toronto. With several members of Gretzky's family down from Brantford for the game, the Oilers were even flatter against the dismal Leafs than they were in Philadelphia against a decent team.

Toronto built a 3-0 edge through one period, just as the Flyers had done two nights earlier, and coasted to a 7-1 verdict. Edmonton's lone goal was by Gretzky, who put a backhander through a screen and past Toronto goalie Michel Larocque.

Larocque played magnificently all night and his stopping of Gretzky on a penalty shot midway through the second period was the highlight of the game. Later, Larocque admitted that the save was the most fulfilling he'd ever made.

In the Edmonton net, Fuhr's 24-game unbeaten streak was conclusively snapped. The rookie hadn't lost since his NHL debut on October 14. This was January 16. Over that stretch, he was 16-0-8.

But Rick Vaive, on his way to the first 50-goal campaign in Maple Leaf history, and Norm Aubin each had two goals in showing Fuhr the rotten side of sports once more.

"I'm not happy about it but it wasn't going to last forever," said Fuhr.

The hours between the debacles in Philadelphia and Toronto seemed to stretch forever for Gretzky. As expected, he was besieged by requests for interviews on this, his only visit to Toronto all season.

On Friday afternoon, after the team had arrived from Philly with a bad taste in its mouth following the poor effort of the previous night, Gretzky was subjected to a news conference which attracted more than 80 writers and broadcasters.

"It was better to get it all out of the way in one swoop than to have Wayne getting no time for himself," reasoned Sather. "Certainly, it's been a distraction. But we can't separate the team and the media. The exposure is good for Canada, for the league and for Edmonton."

So Sather allowed the press its chance at Wayne and, when the interviews were over, he hustled Gretzky to Maple Leaf Gardens.

"Now we can get back to the business at hand," said Sather. "Minus distractions."

But when the Leafs tore apart his club, Sather was blaming "too hard a pace, with too much going on.

"I can't ever remember us playing so poorly," he added. "It was Bad Day at Black Rock and it would've taken more than Spencer Tracy to bail us out."

Game 48, vs. Red Wings at Detroit

The general feeling around the NHL is that Detroit would be a terrific hockey town if only it had a hockey team.

Back in the 50s, the Red Wings were the scourge of the league, winning four Stanley Cups in six years and finishing first in the six-team standings seven years in a row. But Detroit's hockey fortunes have plummeted deeper than Chrysler's stock and the "Dead Wings" have trouble drawing enough people to fill half of Joe Louis Arena's 20,000 seats.

But the Wings, Red or Dead, had no trouble filling the entire building when the Oilers came to town. The largest crowd ever to see a regular season NHL contest, 20,628, showed up for a look at the Great Gretzky.

The fact that the Oilers had played four straight stinkers didn't faze the Detroit brethren a bit. After all, they were used to watching dreadful hockey —the Detroit Dread Wings?—for years.

What they got this time, though, was an inspired effort by the locals, who grabbed a 4-1 lead midway through the game, only to see the Oilers spurt back into a 4-4 tie. The deadlock ended Edmonton's dismal road trip at 0-3-2.

Gretzky helped spark the comeback. At 16:10 of the middle period, he found Coffey at the point and the defenseman rocketed home his 24th goal.

Just 30 seconds into the third session, Gretzky got off his only shot of the night. His 30-footer was stopped by Detroit goalie Bob Sauve, but Hughes pushed in the rebound on a power play to make it 4-3.

Messier, who had scored Edmonton's first goal, knotted it at 14:06 with a 35-footer through a screen.

"I wasn't picking a spot," said Messier, who was the best player on the ice. "I just waited for a screen to form. I think the shot found the short side."

Sather, ever the psychologist, hadn't planned to start Fuhr against the Wings. But after the rookie had lost for the first time in three months the night before, Sather "played him to see what he is made of."

Fuhr was happy with the result.

"It was a bad scene in Toronto," he said. "I was really happy to get another chance to get my confidence back."

Gretzky simply was happy to be heading home.

"This was the worst road trip ever," he said, noting how he'd been hounded by media, well-wishers and even teenage groupies. "I feel like the Beatles."

In a couple of days, he'd be as rich as a Beatle.

Game 49, vs. Blues at Edmonton

What price Gretzky?

Oilers owner Peter Pocklington and Gretzky's representatives had been thrashing that out for months. How much does one pay for the best, especially when the best is getting better and, as far as anyone can tell, will continue to do so?

Just a couple of weeks ago, Gretzky had made some pointed comments about his salary. He wasn't particularly worried about his pay scale, which made him a millionaire and was designed to keep him secure—and with the Oilers—until the end of the century. But he experienced enough annoyance to bring it up.

"I don't want to cut anyone else up or anything," he said, "but why should guys get five times what I do when they're not doing as well as me? I think I do deserve a raise. I signed the contract and I'm obligated to play to that contract. If I was the very first person in the world to renegotiate, I'd say that it's wrong. But everybody does it, in all sports."

Pocklington is a smart man—how else could he have become rich and the employer of the most dominant athlete in the world?—and he was not adverse to renegotiating Wayne's contract. And, when all the numbers were toted up, it came to a nice, round $20 million.

"Wayne could easily make $20 million over the next 15 years," said Pocklington, who promised his young star a shopping center in western Canada after six years. Gretzky also had the option to renegotiate after nine and 15 years.

The base salary of approximately $750,000 a year made Wayne the highest paid player in hockey, easily surpassing the $600,000 earned by Dionne. At that, Pocklington might have been getting off cheap.

"I was offered $2 million for Wayne before he started breaking records," said Pocklington. "I chuckled at the offer and said I wouldn't sell Wayne for $10 million. There is no price on greatness."

Gretzky was relieved that the contract hassling, which began near the start of the season, was over. "It's tough to wake up every morning and read about it," he said. "Now this is out of the way and maybe we can concentrate on nothing but hockey. That's what I'm being paid for, anyway."

The face says it all.

Gretzky was true to his word. That night, he got his sixth hat trick of the season, added two assists and paced a late rally as the Oilers overcame the Blues 8-6.

Edmonton trailed 5-4 when, with sudden power, the Oilers threw four shots past St. Louis goalie Gary Edwards in only 1:41 of the third period.

Gretzky assisted on defenseman Charlie Huddy's first goal of the season 5:48 into the game, then got his 58th at 9:04 by beating Edwards to the short side.

With just under a minute to go in the second period, he broke a 3-3 deadlock with a power-play tally as he outraced Edwards to a loose puck and deposited it into the unguarded cage.

But the Blues jumped into a 5-4 lead halfway through the last period and Edmonton's losing ways seemed to have followed the Oilers back from the road.

Then Tom Roulston, only recently promoted from Wichita, tied the score and, 20 seconds later, Lumley put the Oilers in front.

Gretzky then got No. 60 by shaking off defenseman Bill Baker on a partial breakaway and slapping the puck past Edwards. Only eight seconds later, he fed Anderson to make it 8-5.

"He was looking for me all night and I shot a few times when I felt I should've passed it," said Gretzky of Anderson. "I owed him one.

"Getting 60 doesn't mean that much, really. I got five points too, but I didn't think I played that well. I was tired.

"I know it's part of my job but it's been hectic lately," he noted, thinking of the contract, the road trip and the pressure of filling the spotlight every night. "I'm already looking forward to our five-day break in California."

That wouldn't come for more than a month and it was the furthest thing from Sather's mind.

"As far as I'm concerned, we didn't break out of our slump," said the coach. "We won but I'm not sure we played that well or how bad St. Louis played. The goals-against worry me. We haven't been taking the man off the puck in our end. Too many guys are standing around."

It would be the last time for a long while that Sather would complain about the quality of his team's performance.

Game 50, vs. Canucks at Vancouver

Wayne Gretzky doesn't get mad, he gets even.

At least, where Canucks goalie Richard Brodeur is concerned, Gretzky got more than even.

The night after Gretzky's five-goal effort against Philadelphia which vaulted him to 50 goals, Wayne was blanked by Brodeur in a 3-1 Canuck victory. It was a bad way to spend the last day of what had been a fine year for Gretzky.

This was their next meeting, Game 50. Wayne already had shattered the 50-in-50 plateau and entered this game with 60 goals.

But his non-performance three weeks earlier in Vancouver and some insults Brodeur hurled at him nettled Gretzky. Brodeur, who would go on to playoff glory while Gretzky and the Oilers would flop, had called Wayne "arrogant and a crybaby, a whiner."

Perhaps Brodeur meant winner, because that's what Gretzky would provide in a 4-3 decision for Edmonton.

Blair MacDonald, a former right wing for Gretzky whom Wayne helped score 46 goals in 1979-80, opened the scoring for the Canucks but Roulston tied it a minute later.

Gretzky set up Kurri early in the second period and Hughes beat Brodeur to give the Oilers' a 3-1 cushion. But they let up at the outset of the third period and goals by Darcy Rota and Ivan Hlinka only 33 seconds apart tied it. Brodeur was standing on his head and standing the Oilers on their ears.

With 6½ minutes left, the puck came loose in front of the Vancouver net and Gretzky pounced. His 15-footer won it.

Then he turned his attention to his detractor, Brodeur.

"The puck was just sitting there and I took a swipe," he described. "There's not much else a guy can do when it's that close to the net.

"Brodeur can say what he wants. But maybe he should think before he says things. I think he's just upset because I got on him for his skating out of the net after every save he makes. I told him it was hockey, not figure skating, and he got mad at me."

Having a goalie mad at him did not surprise Gretzky.

"Really," he explained, "the goalies in this league don't seem to like me much."

Game 51, vs. Rockies at Edmonton

Gretzky's last game as a 20-year-old and first at 21, with the usual results: three assists against the Rockies in a 7-4 romp and a goal and an assist to celebrate his birthday in a 6-4 decision over St. Louis.

The Rockies had given Gretzky enough problems early in the season but he had his second consecutive strong game against them with three assists, one in each period. Like a good roommate, Gretzky worked a give-and-go with Lowe and handed the scoring honors to the defenseman.

"This was a night when one team was so intent on stopping Wayne that it forgot what was going on," said Sather. "They (the Rockies) put people all over Wayne and he still got three assists. Meanwhile, the other guys are passing the puck without being checked and skating free.

"Teams spend so much time concentrating on Wayne that they're not prepared for anyone else. That doesn't seem like the way to beat another team. You might stop one guy but we've got others who can carry the load.

"And how often are you going to stop Wayne, anyway?"

Game 52, vs. Blues at St. Louis

As Gretzky celebrated his 21st birthday with a goal and an assist in St. Louis, one could only marvel at how much he had achieved in such a short time.

Wayne first began skating when he was 2. "He took to it like he was born with skates on," said his mother, Phyllis.

Wayne's father, Walter, had built a rink in the family's backyard in Brantford and Wayne's skills flourished so quickly that he was playing on all-star teams with kids twice his age by the time he was 6.

When he was 8, the *Toronto Globe* and *Mail* featured Wayne in a story that said he would change the face of hockey. "This is the next Bobby Orr," the newspaper proclaimed.

At 9, Gretzky was the subject of a Canadian TV special. The next year, he scored an incredible 205 goals, only to surpass that total by 173 the next year.

As a 14-year-old, he left Brantford to wreak havoc on kids still older than him in Toronto. But his final years in Brantford were not his happiest.

"I was 13 and it got to the point where I'd go to the rinks and all I'd hear was 'take his head off. Try to hurt him.' My mom would come home crying after every game.

"It got kind of senseless. Hockey is supposed to be fun and I thought, 'Why keep it up?'

"But nobody wanted me to quit and I didn't want to stop playing. I went to Toronto to get lost in the shuffle of the big city."

At 16, Wayne was playing Junior A at Sault Ste. Marie, where, ironically,

The man who pays the bills, Oilers owner Peter Pocklington.

Esposito grew up. The pros, already drooling in anticipation, were keeping close tabs on this wondrous prospect who scored a hat trick in his junior A contest.

Gretzky spent but one year at the Soo before signing a $1.75 million personal services contract with Nelson Skalbania, owner of the Indianapolis Racers of the WHA. The "new league" had scored a major coup, beating the NHL establishment to the punch on the best hockey prospect since, as the *Globe* and *Mail* so accurately predicted, Mr. Orr.

It was after losing Gretzky to the WHA that the NHL realized it had to get serious about pursuing underaged players. The WHA teams were free to sign kids right out of the cradle, if they so desired. Not long after Gretzky's signing with Indy, the NHL adopted a plan to allow the drafting of junior players previously unavailable because they were too young.

Gretzky's Racer career lasted all of eight games before Skalbania dealt his contract to the Edmonton Oilers. Skalbania, a wheeler-dealer with a history for getting too deep into businesses, then bailing out with a quick profit (or, more recently, heavy losses), found he couldn't afford Gretzky, much less the Racers. Pocklington, seizing one of the best business opportunities in sports history, was only too glad to undertake the expense of employing Gretzky.

On his 18th birthday, Wayne signed a 21-year personal services contract with Pocklington that would net him in the area of $5 million. Three years later, he would ink an updated pact worth four times that.

All of this for doing "the only thing I could ever think of doing when I grew up," said Gretzky. "I'm so lucky to have all this."

Wayne claims he's had only one job in his life.

"I spent a summer working for a highway department and getting up at 6:30 in the morning to shovel gravel," he said. "It was awful. Any time I think back to that and to how my father would tell me that's what I'd be doing if I didn't practice . . . well, that's why you don't hear me complaining about practice.

"You'll never hear me complaining about anything in hockey. Hockey's my life and it's what I've also wanted to be my life."

And now, at 21, Gretzky not only is a hero in Brantford, but throughout Canada and anywhere he travels. They love him in the States and in Europe and even in the Soviet Union. At 21, Gretzky is, to many people, the sport of hockey.

"He's an ambassador of hockey," said Lowe. "He's always thinking for the good of the sport. The demands put on him are unbelievable. In every Eastern city, they tell him it's the only time they'll be able to interview him all year and Wayne lets himself be convinced."

Gretzky's skills as a hockey player are not his sole abilities in athletics. He is a superb baseball player and a terrific lacrosse player.

"To be honest, he has nothing but sports in his head," added Lowe, who knows Gretzky about as well as anyone. "He devours statistics. He could instantly tell you George Brett's batting average, for instance."

And he could recount each of his goals so far this season, including No. 62 against St. Louis. That goal stemmed a tidal wave of scoring by the Blues, who had rallied from 0-5 with three goals in 38 seconds, a team record. Gretzky skated around goalie Gary Edwards to settle matters at 9:49.

Then, he went out for a short birthday celebration before heading to Chicago for the next bit of business.

Game 53, vs. Blacks Hawks at Chicago

Gretzky was once asked whether he let the praise heaped upon him sink in. He shook his head and said simply that he didn't want to get a big head.

He has admitted, however, that when goaltenders pay tribute to him, "It's nice." For Gretzky, that's tantamount to taking several curtain calls.

For more than a decade, Tony Esposito was considered one of the best netminders in the game. He's never led the Black Hawks to a Stanley Cup, but they came close a few times and, without Espo in the net, they wouldn't have threatened anyone. When "Tony O" talks about shooters, people listen.

"Gretzky is great, the best there is," Esposito said after being beaten for Gretzky's 63rd goal, a power-play tally with 8:21 remaining that forced a 3-3 tie. "Nobody handles the puck better or sets up the best shots. He never makes a foolish error. When he's on the ice, a goaltender has to be especially aware.

"There are a lot of times when you can see a play developing," added Espo. "With Gretzky, you never know."

Esposito is in the twilight of his career now, but he was superb against the Oilers with 31 saves. Chicago surged to a 3-2 lead in the third period after being sparked by Esposito's 15 second-period saves. But Chicago gave Gretzky one last chance, which usually is one chance too many.

With 9½ minutes left, the Oilers had possession of the puck in the Hawks' zone and Gretzky broke free in front of the net. Defenseman Doug Wilson managed to tie him up but referee Gregg Madill signaled an interference penalty on Wilson.

About a minute later, Gretzky once again got loose in front of Esposito . . . and he had the puck. He made a couple of fakes—one was all he really needed—then put the puck past a helpless Esposito.

Afterward, Espo was hardly helpless when it came to lauding Gretzky.

"He's in a class by himself, absolutely," said Esposito. "The only guy I've played against or with that I can compare him to is Bobby Orr. I've always considered Orr the best player ever. But Gretzky certainly is in that class, just above all the rest."

"Tony O" included Bobby Hull, Stan Mikita, his brother Phil, Gordie Howe and Jean Beliveau in the superstar category.

"Maybe we need a new description for Gretzky," he concluded.

He winds up . . .
he shoots . . .
he scores.

Sometimes it takes more than your usual goaltending skills to slow down Gretzky.

Game 54, vs. Sabres at Edmonton

Don Edwards, who later would play a crucial role in Gretzky's incredible season, is one of the best goalies in hockey. He showed why in a losing effort, stopping 39 shots and frustrating the Oilers for almost 47 minutes.

But this rapidly maturing bunch from Edmonton displayed its grit by continuing to pressure the Buffalo netminder and finally solving him at 6:47 of the third period.

Hunter's goal tied it: then Gretzky quickly gave the Oilers the lead with his 64th goal. Anderson added an insurance score with just over four minutes remaining and the Oilers skated off with a 3-1 victory on a night when they easily could have lost.

"This is the kind of game which shows how far we've come," said Lowe. "We could have quit with Edwards making all those saves. But we didn't. We kept plugging and turned it our way."

Gretzky hadn't done much but Sabres GM Scotty Bowman was talking about him anyway.

Bowman, who coached the Montreal Canadiens to five Stanley Cups before moving to Buffalo, knows a great player when he sees one. He coached a score of them while with the Canadiens. He's handled dozens more while working with Team Canada in various international competitions. His praise for Gretzky seems to know no bounds.

"Along with Doug Harvey and Bobby Orr," said Bowman, mentioning two of the best—if not the two best—defensemen in league history, "Gretzky's the only guy I've ever seen who has the whole game in his view, as if it was

TITAN
TITAN
CCM

A workingman's smile.

being played on TV, in slow motion. and he's doing it from up front.

"I can remember a game we had last year with Edmonton. We were leading 7-5. Gretzky had the puck inside his own blue line and he went through three of our guys in a space of 15 feet and then beat our goaltender. We had a good defensive team at the time and I was furious at our guys. I thought they'd goofed.

"But then I saw him another time in a crowd in front of the net put the puck on the sticks of four of his teammates in 15 seconds. Four scoring opportunities in 15 seconds! Can you believe it?

"Now, he's got the whole league mesmerized. They're on the defensive before he comes out of his own zone."

Bowman's speech would replay in the mind just three weeks later when the Oilers paid their only visit to upstate New York. That would be mesmerizing.

Game 55, vs. Flyers at Edmonton

For one period, the lumbering Flyers (who are remarkably devoid of flying skaters) looked as if they could almost stay with the fleet Oilers. Twenty minutes does not a hockey game make, however.

After one period, the Oilers led 3-2 and Gretzky had popped his 65th goal on a backhander that eluded Flyers goalie Rick St. Croix. He and Kurri also had combined to set up Anderson on a power play late in the period.

Edmonton exploded for three goals in the first eight minutes of the next period and the Flyers were dead. Wayne got No. 66 when Coffey fed him at the crease and he stuffed the puck in. He assisted on a goal by Kurri when he won a faceoff and sent the puck to Anderson in the corner. Andy fired it in front to Kurri, who beat a defenseless St. Croix.

Gretzky's third goal of the game and 13th in his last four meetings with Philly, came on a 20-foot drive. Had St. Croix not robbed him on a breakaway, Gretzky would have had yet another four-goal night.

The line of Gretzky-Kurri-Anderson was devastating. In addition to Wayne's three goals and two assists, Anderson had a goal and two assists and Kurri chipped in a goal and an assist. Gretzky had an almost unfathomable 12 shots on goal.

"That line made us look like we'd never been coached," said Quinn, who must have been getting used to such Edmonton hijinks. "We'd go here and put out a fire, there and put out a fire. We were backing off and you sure can't do that with Gretzky. It's bad to do against anyone in the NHL. But against Gretzky . . .

"It has always been my opinion that team play can eliminate or at least neutralize a great individual talent," added Quinn, who was without spectacular talents on his roster. "Maybe not."

As for Gretzky, he was fast approaching all kinds of scoring marks. If he could have found a way to keep the Flyers in town for a few more games, those records would have been his in no time.

"I'm sure he'd like to play against us for 80 games," said Quinn, who probably felt like barfing at the thought.

Game 56, vs. Canadiens at Edmonton

The proud Canadiens were tired of hearing about last spring, about how the upstart Oilers, this bunch from the WHA, of all places, had swept the Canadiens right out of the playoffs. How, for the second straight year, they had failed to bring home what Montrealers consider their birthright, the Stanley Cup.

It didn't help their outlook that, in their home city, Gretzky was the most popular player. No. 99 jerseys sold at about a 2-to-1 ratio to those of Lafleur or Larry Robinson or any of the local heroes.

"When we all went home in the summer," said Lowe, "no matter where we went, people told us we were their favorite team. They said we were the next Cup team, maybe for several years to come.

"It all happened because we beat Montreal. They played 'The Impossible Dream' before the games here in Edmonton and everyone started believing. That's a main reason we're in first place now."

The No. 1 reason, of course, was Gretzky. Canadiens broadcaster Danny Gallivan, who has seen nearly all of the game's superstars and described their phenomenal skills, has had special pleasure watching Gretzky.

"There are a lot of other good hockey players in the NHL," said Gallivan. "People like Bossy, Trottier, Dionne and Peter Stastny. But Gretzky has left them far behind in goals and total points. Opposing players would hit him if they could. They can't get a good piece of him because he sees them coming and he has such quick reflexes.

"Some of us were talking about him before a game and one guy said that he scored over 60 percent of his goals in the third period. He thought it was because the opposing team's pre-game plan was to check him closely but as the game wore on, they grew a little careless and, boom, the puck was in the net."

Doug Jarvis, the pesky Canadiens' center who drew the dubious chore of shadowing Gretzky, agreed that a team's game plan wasn't always carried out for 60 minutes, and Gretzky is the first and best at taking advantage of any letups. Those letups don't necessarily have to be by the man checking him, either.

"Certainly Gretzky is tough to defend for a center," said Jarvis. "But everybody on the ice has a problem. When he goes behind the net like he does, either you have to jump on him right away or tie up his wingers in front of the net. I like the idea of jumping on him immediately if I can."

Jarvis is more familiar with Gretzky than most NHL players. When he was playing Junior B, Jarvis' coach was none other than Walter Gretzky, Wayne's father.

"Wayne plays like most offensive centers in that he is always in position to break out of his own end when he gets the puck," said Jarvis. "He tends to draw guys to him but you can't get sucked in because then you're inviting him to make a pass to an open man. If he has an open man, he'll find him and hit him.

"He's always the guy who starts the play, the guy who makes the pass. Of course, now that's been his reputation but he's decided to shoot more this year and look what he's done. So he's always adding something to his game.

"He'll draw a lot of penalties too, because he is covered so closely. When they get on the power play, they're really tough. You have to play conservative against Edmonton."

The Canadiens were at their stingiest—and most explosive—in the first period, outshooting the Oilers 21-5 and grabbing a 3-1 margin. It was 3-0 after 13 minutes but Gretzky got away from Jarvis long enough to set up Anderson late in the period.

When Wayne took a feed from Coffey and slammed the puck behind Montreal goalie Rick Wamsley in the last minute of the second period, the Oilers were within a goal despite being outplayed all the way and outshot 24-11.

The final period belonged, totally, to the Canadiens, who scored their first triumph over the Oilers in more than a year. Mark Napier scored twice and Steve Shutt got his second goal of the game as Montreal chalked up a 6-3 win. It was the first loss for the Oilers in nine games and would be their last defeat for a month, spanning 11 games and a slew of records by Gretzky.

Montreal's strategy, which basically called for Jarvis to attach himself to Gretzky's personage and follow him along every inch of the ice, worked well. Even Jarvis was impressed by that.

"I think the score shows we did a pretty good job," he said. "Gretzky makes everybody around him better and everybody on our team has to play his best because of it. Just when you think you've got him, he's got you. He's not only hard to catch and check, he's hard to predict. The best you can do is force him into the lowest percentage position possible, then hope."

Game 57, vs. Maple Leafs at Edmonton

Games against the Maple Leafs can be a lot of laughs. Toronto is the kind of team that can rise above its mediocrity only in spurts. More often, however, the Leafs play on a level so far below other NHL clubs that they'd have trouble making the playoffs in the AHL or CHL.

Still, the Oilers had been knocked on their butts by the Leafs in their last meeting. That stuck in Sather's craw.

"Glen was pretty intense before the game," said Lowe. "He really wanted us to win, I guess to make up for the game in Toronto."

It was questionable whether Gretzky was getting enough time to concentrate on his hockey. National magazines such as *Newsweek*, *Time*, and *Sports Illustrated* were working on features on The Great Gretzky. All three U.S. television networks were planning features about him on their news magazine shows.

"The mass media has a thirst for something like a Wayne Gretzky," said NHL President John Ziegler. "The spectacular aspect of his record-breaking performances brought attention to the league and the game from people and organizations that were not necessarily even casual fans. He extended the awareness of our sport in North America and all over the world."

With all this attention and all the demands for his time, Gretzky still managed to perform miracles on the ice.

He wasn't especially magical against Toronto, but he contributed two assists, on goals by Kurri and Messier, who scored a pair. The Leafs were their usual placid, disinterested selves and ended up with just 19 shots at Low. The Oilers coasted to a 5-1 victory.

"That was one of the easier games a goalie can expect," offered Low. "By the time they put on any pressure, it was 4-0."

In many ways, this game was typical of the 1981-82 Oilers. The only unusual thing, perhaps, was that Gretzky did not put one into the net. But he agreed that this was straight out of the mold as far as Edmonton hockey games went this season.

"So many times, we'd jump on teams and get up 3-0 and they'd have no choice but to open it up and we'd get more chances," he said. "We were up 2-0 tonight with less than four minutes gone. That had to change the Leafs' thinking."

Game 58, vs. Rangers at Edmonton

The last game before the All-Star break and already the Oilers were in the playoffs. They clinched a spot without much fanfare in an 8-4 decision over the Rangers.

Although the league keeps no such records, it was believed that the February 7 clinching date was the earliest a team had ever qualified for the playoffs.

Gretzky entered the contest with slightly mixed emotions. In goal for the Rangers was Ed Mio, one of Wayne's closest friends in hockey.

"He took care of me in Indy," said Gretzky, referring to his short stay with the WHA Racers. "I was 17 and the drinking age was 21, so we'd go over to Eddie's house for a few beers."

Mio was involved in the same transaction which sent Gretzky from Indianapolis to Edmonton. He also was the Oilers' top goalie until breaking a finger late last season. When Moog starred in the playoffs, then Fuhr was drafted on the first round, there was no room for Mio.

He was demoted to Wichita and, in mid-December, with the Rangers down to only rookie goalies in their entire organization, they traded center Lance Nethery to the Oilers for him.

Mio looked forward to playing the Oilers and to proving that Sather erred in getting rid of him.

"Going down to Wichita hurt because I knew I could still do the job in Edmonton," said Mio. "I had been the No. 1 goalie or shared it with Ronnie (Low) and I thought I earned better treatment. But when they drafted Fuhr, I knew there wouldn't be much playing time here.

TITAN

99
OILERS
CANADIEN
CANADIEN
TITAN

The three stages to a goal:
possession (upper left)
preparation (lower left)
power (above).

"I'm over my bitterness. I think I'd still be bitter if I was in Wichita. My lip was really on the ground there."

Both Mio and Gretzky admitted they weren't anxious to face one another.

"Wayne's one of my closest friends," said Mio. "But if you try treating one guy different, you screw things up. I think we both realize that and have to try to treat this like any other game and treat each other like any other player."

"When I go one-on-one with Eddie, he's not going to let me score," Gretzky said. "You don't have any friends in the other uniform during a game."

Mio did not show much to change Sather's mind. Perhaps it was nerves or a preoccupation with showing up the Oilers' management. Or maybe it was just another example of the Edmonton machine taking apart a defense and a goaltender. But Mio played his worst game as a Ranger.

Gretzky assisted on Fogolin's first-period goal and made it 7-4 with his 69th tally in the third period. But he wasn't on the ice for the goal which destroyed the Rangers' chances.

After New York rallied from a three-goal hole to within 5-4, Siltanen took the puck in center ice and sent in a high, bouncing shot. He then headed for the bench but, before he'd gotten off the ice, the crowd let out a tremendous roar. Mio had lost the puck in the lights and it bounded past him and into the net.

"I blew it," said Mio. "I let the team down on that goal."

Gretzky wasn't about to criticize his buddy. Instead, he spoke about the success Mio was having in New York.

"I'm glad Eddie's been doing well," he said. "I kept telling people that last year; we won 30 games and he won 18 of them. (Actually, it was 16 of 29.)

"Eddie is a terrific goalie and the Rangers are lucky to have him."

The Oilers were headed for a four-day break but Gretzky, Fuhr, Coffey and Messier journeyed to Washington, D.C., for the All-Star Game.

Game 59, vs. Capitals at Edmonton

Gretzky was thinking about Washington, which seemed fitting since the Capitals were in town. But his mind was on the city, where he had just performed in the All-Star Game—scoring a goal on a second-period breakaway—and sat at the head table for a White House luncheon hosted by President Reagan.

Sometimes, Wayne Gretzky forgets who Wayne Gretzky is and what he has done the last few years.

"He gets awed by meeting some of these people," said Messier. "But he's one of them. It's OK for me or some of the rest of us to be in awe when you meet the president of the U.S. or Bob Hope, but Wayne's a star too. He forgets that."

Adds Lowe, "Gretz calls me in the off-season and says things like, 'Gee, I just met Bob Hope and he wants me to be on his show.' Or 'I'm gonna be on a Paul Anka special, can you believe it?' All of us can believe it but for Gretz, it's hard to believe. He doesn't rank himself with those stars."

Certainly, President Reagan did. Each of the NHL All-Stars and several league and team officials were greeted by the president in a reception line prior to the luncheon. When Wayne reached Reagan, the president first spoke with him, then took him aside and introduced him to Vice President Bush. Gretzky was the only person to receive such treatment.

Then Wayne joined the president, Hope, NHL president Ziegler, Gordie Howe, Esposito and the Canadian ambassador to the U.S. at the head table.

"All I could remember was what Gordie told me a couple of years ago," a beaming Gretzky said later. "He told me the Lord gave you two ears and one mouth for a reason. Well, I just sat there and listened. I think I put that suggestion to very good use."

Reagan paid tribute to hockey as a sport which "requires a special breed of athlete," and also mentioned the beauty and artistry which is an integral

On February 8, 1982, President Reagan addresses a White House luncheon for the National Hockey League as Vice President Bush listens on. At far right is Wayne Gretzky of the Edmonton Oilers.

part of the sport. Then he turned his attention to Gretzky.

"I'm told our local team, the Washington Capitals, was interested in trading for Wayne," Reagan said. "They were told the price was two first-round draft choices and the state of Texas."

With those tributes fresh in his mind, Gretzky went out and contributed three points to a 5-3 win over the Caps.

He became only the second player ever to score 70 goals in the regular season when he poked in Kurri's pass at 9:02 of the second period. Then he set up Messier on a power play to boost the Oilers into a 3-3 tie early in the third stanza and, after Hagman pushed the Oilers in front at 14:06, he assisted on Coffey's wrapup goal just 31 seconds later.

Edmonton fired 51 shots at beleaguered goalie Dave Parro. The Oilers looked fresh and vigorous all night and only Parro's work kept Washington close.

By now, the likelihood of breaking Esposito's 76-goal mark had become a certainty. The only questions were where and when and how many Gretzky would wind up with.

"A couple of seasons ago, I really enjoyed going for individual things," he said. "But it wasn't all that much fun because we were losing. Now that we're winning, it's really become fun again.

"Chasing records doesn't mean much when your team is bad. But if those records are helping you win, then let them come.

"If there was ever a record which seemed impossible to break, I think it was Phil's record of 76 goals. You get guys come close, like Bossy did last year. But he only got to 68."

Gretzky was past that and, with 21 games left, the countdown to 76 and beyond had begun.

99
99
PROFES
CANADA
W GRETZKY

Game 60, vs. Bruins at Edmonton

The last time the Oilers hooked up with the Bruins, they allowed Boston new life and three late goals propelled the Bruins into a 4-4 tie. This time, Edmonton did the rallying, with Lumley connecting in the final two minutes to secure a 2-2 deadlock.

The Oilers proved they could play the style of game the Bruins prefer—tight checking and hard but clean hitting—and not be overwhelmed. And they proved they can avoid defeat even when Gretzky is having an off night.

Off nights are a way of life for Gretzky when he faces the Bruins. Wayne was headed for all kinds of offensive records within the next six weeks but if he had to face Boston and Kasper more often, he might not win the scoring title.

For the third time during the season, Kasper held his own against Gretzky. In fact, it was Kasper who put Boston up a goal 6:17 into the game.

Anderson, with help from Gretzky and defenseman Gary Lariviere, tied it in the second period, but Brad Park whistled a power-play shot past Fuhr at 6:18 of the third. Lumley's late goal earned the Oilers a point.

After the game, Kasper was besieged by reporters for some tips on the secret to nullifying Wayne Gretzky. Surely other coaches and general managers in the league would soon follow, notebooks and tape recorders in hand, for whatever tidbits they could gather from Kasper the Checker.

"It's a bump and grind kind of thing," said Kasper, who clinched the Selke Trophy as the NHL's top defensive forward with his handling of a man nobody else in the league could come within light years of slowing down. "I try to keep myself between him and the puck so that if they pass to him, it has to come through me. even if he does get it, he's usually outside, where he's not as dangerous.

"When he's got the puck, you have to keep close to him as you can. He can accelerate quickly, so I try to bump him off stride. Of course, he tries to bump me off his tail, too.

"Then, when he gets behind the net, you have to arrive there at the same time, either to try to bump him off the puck or tie him up any way you can."

"I'd have to say he does a better job on me than anyone else," said Gretzky, admitting the obvious. "In my mind, he certainly deserves the Selke. But I think he owes me half of it.

"He plays the angles so well, like a center in basketball. He cuts off the angle before I can get to the net. He doesn't give me a lane to get to the net and gets help when I go somewhere else to make a move towards the net."

"It seems I get more publicity for what I do against Gretzky than what I do against other teams," said Kasper. "I like to think from my success against other teams and not just what I did against Gretzky, I earned the award. It shouldn't be based just on three games against Gretzky."

When Kasper was in juniors, he shadowed people like Denis Savard, now a high-scoring center with the Chicago Black Hawks. So he had lots of practice at it before coming to Boston.

But it takes a lot more than practice to be able to neutralize someone who is destroying everyone else.

"People don't think shadows have to be smart," noted Cheevers. "They couldn't be more wrong."

Added Cashman, "Steve is so good at it because he's got the heart of a lion. He gives you 100 percent every game, whether you're ahead 10-1 or down 10-1, whether it's close or a runaway. He is completely unselfish and willing to sacrifice himself for the team. There are very few guys like Steve around any more."

To which Gretzky would add a hearty, "Amen."

Game 61, vs. North Stars at Edmonton

Don Beaupre, who had been in goal three months earlier when Gretzky had a rare pointless night, would not be so charmed this time.

Gretzky got five more points on this February night. He scored twice and set up three goals as Edmonton broke open a close contest with three quick scores in the third stanza.

The real star of the night was Messier. His hat trick boosted him to 40 goals for the season.

"I feel as if I've gotten better each season," noted Messier. "I wasn't a big scorer in the WHA and I didn't start out with the Oilers getting a lot of points and goals.

"But I've gotten more ice time and more confidence. And I've gotten to play a lot with Gretz."

And that's the key. Get as much time on the ice with Gretzky centering for you as possible and the points will keep right on coming. Remember Lumley?

But don't shortchange Messier, either. He has a wicked shot and is a strong skater who can take punishment. His knack around the net is surpassed on the Oilers by no one except Gretzky.

The North Stars led 2-0 after a period and Messier fought with Minnesota defenseman Gary Sargent. Gretzky started the Edmonton comeback at 6:48 of the second period, slicing the deficit to one with a hard slapshot, using Sargent as a screen. Siltanen had spotted Gretzky clear enough to get off a shot and Wayne didn't hesitate, beating Beaupre over his catching glove .

A minute and a half later, Gretzky made the best play of the night. He used his skate to knock down a pass at the Minnesota blue line and fed Anderson at the side of the net. Andy had no trouble depositing the puck behind Beaupre.

Minnesota grabbed another lead on a goal by Craig Hartsburg; then Gretzky outskated three North Stars at the blue line and fed Lowe at the side of the cage to tie it again. Messier then got his first of the night and added his second early in the final period.

Gretzky's 72nd goal interrupted Messier's personal run. Again Wayne used a blistering slapshot—something critics claimed he didn't possess just a year ago—for No. 72. Messier closed out the blitz with his third goal of the game.

Earlier , Fuhr had to yield to Low when his shoulder again popped out. Twice that night it was pushed back into place and Fuhr would be out of the lineup for only a week.

Beaupre, who had walked around the dressing room at the 1981 All-Star Game, in which he played goal, and asked each player for his autograph, was awed by Gretzky.

"The guy doesn't give you a second to think," said Beaupre. "Those two slapshots were out of cannons. How does anybody stop those?"

Wayne had one game remaining at home, against Hartford, before the Oilers started a long road trip. He was four goals shorts of Esposito's 76 but was within a small step of his own points mark of 164—he had 161.

"Sure, I'd like to break the record at home but I know it'll be tough," he said. "But I play on a team that isn't selfish and they'll pass the puck over."

Game 62
vs. Whalers at Edmonton

When Greg Millen left the Penguins as a free agent prior to this season, he didn't have many takers, even though his name already was in the NHL record books.

Millen, the young goalie who nearly willed the Penguins to an upset of St. Louis in the opening round of the 1981 playoffs—the Blues won the series in double overtime in the decisive fifth game—wound up signing with Hartford. The Whalers ignored that notation in the record book.

"It's not something I always want to be remembered for," said the aggressive netminder. "I hope I achieve things in hockey that erase that from peoples' minds."

On March 29, 1981, Millen was in goal when Gretzky broke Esposito's points record of 152. Wayne was on his way to 164 points and the Oilers' itinerary placed them in Pittsburgh when it came time for Gretzky to establish a new points mark.

Less than 11 months later, Gretzky stood on the verge of another points record. And Millen stood in the Hartford net, hoping history wouldn't repeat itself.

In sports, though, history has a way of doing precisely that. The great athletes, the Earl Campbells, Mike Schmidts and Julius Ervings, often return to the scene of the crime for more memorable accomplishments.

In a way, that's what was happening with Gretzky on February 19, 1982. It was Millen's misfortune to be in the way. Again.

"You'd think he'd have some mercy on an old teammate," kidded Millen, who played with Gretzky at the Soo. But he knew better. And Wayne didn't wait long to begin his assault on his own 164-point mark.

Midway through the opening period, Gretzky set up Anderson on a 2-on-1 for Andy's 30th goal of the campaign on a tip-in. Five minutes later, Gretzky split defensemen Blake Wesley and Mickey Volcan and whistled a slapshot that went through Millen's logo.

That gave Gretzky 163 points. Next up, the record-equalizer.

Only 1:42 into the second period, Gretzky found the red-hot Kurri on a 2-on-1 break on a power play. Gretzky raced down left wing, waited for

Wesley to come to him and fed Kurri for a tip-in.

Of course, Gretzky wasn't nearly finished with the Whalers or his former teammate. At 11:28, he took a pass from Kurri on yet another 2-on-1 and slid the puck just inside the post for his 74th goal and a new points record.

For good measure, Gretzky outmaneuvered Millen in the third period as the Oilers romped 7-4. He took a pass from Messier and, standing at the lip of the goal crease, slid his 75th goal under Millen.

"I tried to pokecheck Gretzky but I missed it," said Millen. "I knew where it was going after that."

With the game well in hand, the Oilers started pressing to feed Wayne for his 76th to tie Espo.

"We knew Wayne was going to get 76 and more," said Anderson. "We thought it would have been great to get it at home."

With 15 seconds left and the sellout crowd on its feet, screaming encouragement, Gretzky got his chance. It would be the only one he'd get at home to tie Espo because the Oilers would begin an eight-game road trip two nights later in Detroit.

"Glenn threw it out but one of the Whalers must have gotten a stick on it," said Gretzky. "It knuckled on me. I hit it and it popped into the air."

And out of harm's way. The final buzzer sounded with Gretzky at 75 goals and 166 points.

"I don't think it means that much to break your own record," he said. "You kind of expect to progress, which means you will do it."

He was a little disappointed that he couldn't at least tie with Espo in Edmonton. But he wasn't exactly crushed.

"I had my chances but it just wasn't meant to be," said Gretzky. "I'll just have to go for it in Detroit."

Game 63, vs. Red Wings at Detroit

In the 65-year history of the National Hockey League, only one man had ever scored 76 goals in a season. That man was Esposito, who was among the 20,270 spectators at Joe Louis Arena expecting to see a second player put a 76th puck into the enemy net.

Gretzky's pace was so torrid that he seemed headed for a 100-goal, 230-point campaign. For now, however, only No. 76 was on his mind.

It also was foremost in the mind of Wings coach Wayne Maxner, who spent a great deal of time before the game toying with several defenses designed to thwart Gretzky. He ended up opting for use of his best checker, speedy Paul Woods, as a shadow for Gretzky, with the Detroit defensemen offering a helping hand—and skate and stick and whatever else was available—whenever possible.

Wayne spent much of the first minute of the game flat on the ice, the victim of hard checks and, with only 28 seconds gone, an interference penalty against Woods.

At 4:02, with the Oilers on another power play, Gretzky gave Anderson a perfect feed and the Oilers moved on top. The period ended that way, but not before goalie Bob Sauve robbed Gretzky late in the session with a quick pad save.

The crowd, which seemed divided in loyalties between the horrible hometowners and the exciting visitors, was on Gretzky's side whenever he took the ice. The fans were far more involved in the contest than most Detroit spectators ever get. The average Wings' crowd was less than half what the Oilers had attracted through the turnstiles. Those extra 10,000 fans were on hand hoping to see an historic event. They didn't want the local team standing in the way.

Eight minutes into the second period, Gretzky outraced defenseman Jim

Schoenfeld to the puck behind the Wings' net and sent a pass to the point, where Lowe was waiting. His slapshot sailed past Sauve for a 2-0 Edmonton edge.

After Mark Osborne connected for Detroit, Gretzky got his third assist of the game, threading a pass through Detroit's Walt McKechnie to Messier.

Kurri scored on another Gretzky pass at 8:16 of the final period, giving Wayne four assists. But beautiful passes and playmaking craftmanship were not what the fans had flocked to see.

Gretzky had managed five shots but Sauve was equal to all of them. It appeared the lowly Red Wings would hold Gretzky goalless, and the chase of Esposito would move on to Buffalo with Wayne still at 75.

Then Detroit defenseman John Barrett was penalized with 5:42 remaining, bringing a rather robust cheer from the spectators. Surely Gretzky would connect now. Surely his teammates would set him up until he dropped from shooting or beat Sauve. Surely they will not have watched in vain.

Sorry. The Red Wings, though hopelessly behind, killed the penalty.

Seconds after Barrett emerged from the box and many of the fans gave up hope, Anderson took the puck near the Detroit blue line.

"I dumped it into the corner to get around (defenseman) Reed Larson," said Anderson. "He came to me. There was only one guy to give it to. (Eric) Vail and Schoenfeld were standing between myself and Wayne and they were checking him well. Maybe they thought there was no way I was going to get the pass to him. It was like a 'I got him, you got him' thing."

But nobody had him. Gretzky had been cruising in center ice but broke for the net when he saw Anderson send the puck into the left wing corner.

"Andy is noted for barrelling into situations," Gretzky explained. "I knew there was an excellent chance he'd be the first one to get to the puck. They paid attention to him and I think they forgot about me."

Anderson didn't, sending a perfect pass in front. Gretzky banged in a 10-foot shot, the crowd exploded, Wayne shot his gloved fist into the air and No. 76 was in the books.

"I'd had my chances before," he said. "This time, I couldn't miss after the pass Andy gave me.

"I thought Woods did a good job. We did a lot of skating tonight and he stuck to me pretty good. When a guy shadows you that closely, you rarely get time to release the puck quickly. That's not one of my biggest assets . . . I can't release it quick like a Bossy."

But he was doing something . . . a lot of things . . . right. It had taken only 284 shots to reach 76 goals, meaning he scored on almost one-quarter of his shots.

Esposito, who works as a television commentator for the Rangers, didn't seem disturbed that he'd have to follow Gretzky to Buffalo—or beyond to see his record broken.

"I wanted to be here and I want to be wherever he scores his 77th," said Espo. "When I broke Bobby Hull's record (58 goals) that year I wound up with 76, I wished he could have been there to see it. I was coming to Detroit whether the NHL said to or not. I'll be in Buffalo whether they ask me to or not."

Gretzky was a bit embarrassed by the fanfare.

"When I heard Phil and Mr. Ziegler were coming, I think it added a little pressure," he said with a smile. "I don't want them to have to follow me over the country until I get it. I don't want to keep them away from their business."

Which meant Gretzky would get down to business, the business of breaking the goals record, in Buffalo.

Against Buffalo, Wayne only has eyes for the puck.

Game 64, vs. Sabres at Buffalo

With Goal No. 76 in the ledger, just about the entire sporting world began to follow Gretzky's exploits, hoping to share the magic moment that would catapult him ahead of Esposito.

The game in Buffalo was sold out a month in advance, well before anyone knew that it might be a historic night.

Gretzky had two days to savor the goal in Detroit, which came on a Sunday night. The contest in Buffalo was on Wednesday, February 24. For some folks on the brink of shattering a record previously considered unapproachable, the wait might seem like an eternity. For Gretzky, it was a chance to go back to Brantford, to "sit around and do absolutely nothing" for a while.

So as the media descended on Buffalo from everywhere in North America, hoping to get a few pearls of wisdom from Gretzky, and scalpers began asking as much as $75 a ticket for the game, Wayne made the 100-minute drive to Brantford.

"It was a real good chance to relax," he said. "I went to my brothers' schools. A couple of kids in Glenn's class were doing speeches on me. I just sat in the back and had a good time."

The Oilers allowed one hour of interviews with Gretzky that Tuesday after practice. As usual, he was patient and cooperative, though he did mention that "it seems like a lot of folks who don't know that much about hockey" were asking him questions. Those questions ranged from his personal habits away from the rink to his girl friend, entertainer Vickie Moss, to his contract. Gretzky handled the queries without breaking stride, as if the interviewers were simply enemy defensemen he had to stickhandle past.

It seemed that nearly every other question asked of Wayne—when the questions dealt with hockey—was about his feelings concerning breaking Espo's record away from Edmonton.

"Sure, I'd like to have done it at home," he repeated for, oh, the 77th time. "I tried but, if it has to come on the road, Buffalo is a great place. It's close to my home and my father will be there to see it.

"There isn't anything you can do about the schedule. At least, by going after it in Buffalo, my family is nearby."

Gretzky's record chase wasn't the only significant sporting event taking place in Buffalo. The Major Indoor Soccer League was holding its All-Star Game the night before the Oilers-Sabres game at Memorial Auditorium.

The MISL is struggling for fans and recognition for the newfangled version of the world's most popular sport. Though Gretzky's presence in Buffalo was front page—as in first page of the entire newspaper—news, the MISL game was getting plenty of ink, too.

The league tried to get Gretzky to kick out the first ball, a ceremony he was no stranger to.

"I'd love to do it," Gretzky said when approached, though he knew he'd have to get permission from Pocklington, permission that never came because Pocklington owns the Edmonton Drillers team in the North American Soccer League, a rival to the MISL. "I did it once with the Drillers and I missed the empty net. I shot it wide of that big, goddamn net. Maybe it was too big."

Obviously, Gretzky's scoring touch does not carry over to soccer.

"Yeah, but I'd love to play in that league," he said with a sly smile creasing his face. "All they do is score like crazy."

Gretzky also considered going to see Brian Bellows, a junior player being touted as—what else?—the "next Gretzky," play in Fort Erie, a few miles from Buffalo. Gretzky was having no trouble relaxing.

"Why not relax?" he asked. "I think I'm going to get one more goal this season. I don't see any reason to be uptight about it."

Getting that goal against the Sabres and Edwards, their All-Star goalie, would be no picnic.

"I think I've scored twice on Donnie and one was into an empty net after they pulled him," said Gretzky. "We were teammates on Team Canada and I got to watch him a lot. Donnie's one of the most underrated goalies in the league. He's also one of the best. He stays on his feet more than any goalie in the league. He makes you commit yourself or he forces you to take the shot he wants you to take, not always the one you're looking for.

"When you get one goal past him, you're doing well."

One goal was all Wayne needed for the record, however, and Edwards was as aware of it as anyone. Asked if he would mind being the goalie who gave up No. 77—as long as the Sabres beat the Oilers—Edwards shrugged.

"If we win," he said, "I guess I don't care much who gets goals for them."

"But I won't be just concentrating on Gretzky. I have a whole team to worry about and if I just look to stop one guy, Gretzky or anybody, I'm not being fair to my team. I'll play my regular game."

A majority of the crowd arrived early at the Aud, some to hang banners lauding their local heroes, others to display handiwork praising No. 99. Gretzky received an ovation when he skated out for warmups and a big cheer rang out when he put a practice shot into the net past Fuhr.

When the game began, though, it was clear that the fans were in the Aud to see a Sabres' victory. Gretzky could score as many as he liked as long as Buffalo won. But most of the fans seemed willing to satisfy themselves with one Gretzky score for the record, and plenty of Sabres' goals.

The goal-scoring record wasn't the only one Gretzky had his sights zeroed in on. He entered the game with 171 points, on his way to 200. Scoring 100 points in a season was a dream until Esposito achieved it with 126 in 1968-69. Doubling that was, before Gretzky, the dream of a madman.

Wayne pushed closer to 200 without taking any dangerous shots in the first 20 minutes. In fact, the only shot he got in the opening period was a weak one that Edwards could have stopped blindfolded.

Gretzky set up two goals as the Oilers grabbed a 3-1 margin through a period. On the first Edmonton goal of the game, Gretzky won a faceoff and sent the puck back to Huddy at the left point. Huddy's shot, though not particularly hard, fooled Edwards.

With the Oilers leading 2-1 later in the stanza, Gretzky and Kurri broke up ice on a 2-on-1. In such situations, the defenseman who is back often tries to get the puck-carrier to shoot, mainly because the goalie must always concentrate on the man with the puck and has a better chance of stopping a shot if no passes are involved.

But this was Wayne Gretzky lugging the puck and, cognizant of that fact —and of the possibility that here was Goal No. 77 about to be planted in the Buffalo net—the Sabres let Kurri skate freely to Edwards' right. The goalie challenged Gretzky who, at the last possible second, passed to Kurri for a shot into and unguarded cage.

Buffalo scored the only goal of the second period but Gretzky created plenty of excitement. He had three excellent opportunities to deposit the monumental goal behind Edwards. All three times, the goalie got the better of the duel.

Early in the period, after some loose play along the boards in the Sabres' zone, the puck came to Gretzky. He unleashed a 25-foot slapshot, his most effective weapon for much of the season, but Edwards stabbed it with his glove.

A bit later, Gretzky sneaked through traffic and suddenly was bearing in on Edwards, with a checker desperately trying to halt his progress. Gretzky got off a quick backhander that Edwards knocked away.

As the period wound down, Gretzky again got himself free for a slapshot from the top of the slot. The puck bounced off Edwards' leg pad.

Early in the final period, the Sabres tied it as veteran Gil Perreault—the only original Sabre still playing for the team—scored for the third time. It was the 12th hat trick of Perreault's illustrious career and placed him squarely in the spotlight, with, for the moment, Gretzky's pursuit of the goals record shunted aside.

(Ironically, Perreault had been honored in a pre-game ceremony for becoming the Sabres' all-time leading scorer, a ploy by Bowman to fire up his star and his team. And a ploy which was working.)

With the game knotted, No. 77 became somewhat secondary for the Oilers. To a man, they said before the game that Gretzky's setting the record would not block out their chief aim: to win. There would be plenty more nights for Wayne to get 77.

Of course, the Oilers' best chance for winning is to give the puck to Gretzky and let him perform tricks with it.

At 6:42 of the period, the Oilers tricked Buffalo into getting caught up ice. Once again, Gretzky broke free on a 2-on-1 with Anderson. After a give-and-go, there stood Gretzky to the right of the slot, with a gaping net before him. He shot, a quick wrist shot that had No. 77 written on it. Edwards dived head-first and deflected the puck with his glove.

It was one of the best opportunities Gretzky had had all season with converting. If he couldn't put that one in, he probably wasn't going to put any by Edwards this night.

Gretzky took a couple more shifts but didn't come close to scoring. He seemed a bit withdrawn on the ice, not as quick or opportunistic as usual.

"In the first and second period, I was a little draggy," he noted. "In the third, I was at a point where I was so tired; then I got my second wind."

One of the marks of his greatness is his ability to appear out of nowhere, the puck in his possession, the goalie at his mercy. It is in this way that Gretzky differs most from Orr or Hull, men who so dominated the flow of the game that you couldn't help but notice them, no matter what they were doing. Gretzky, on the other hand, materializes out of thin air, like an apparition, does his damage, then disappears.

When Sabres right wing Steve Patrick—who, along with Craig Ramsay, Dale McCourt and several other Sabres was used to check Gretzky—mishandled the puck near his blue line, Gretzky was there. He grabbed the puck, glided around Patrick with ease and, with defenseman Richie Dunn hooking him to distract him, Wayne Gretzky became the greatest single season goal-scorer in hockey history. He slid a wrist shot under Edwards.

"My first thought was that it put us ahead 4-3," said Gretzky of the record-setter. "Then, as I turned to stride to the corner, I felt relief and satisfaction. It's a lot of pressure off me."

The rest of the Oilers stormed across the rink to mob Gretzky. The crowd of 16,433, forgetting loyalties, saluted Gretzky with loud applause and a standing ovation.

From his seat at center ice, Esposito raised a fist in the air and exclaimed, "All right!" He then made his way to the public address announcer's booth and presented the puck to "the most talented and one of the nicest guys in hockey.

"Wayne," added Esposito, "thank you for letting me be a part of this."

There was still 6:36 remaining and for those final 396 seconds, Gretzky put on a clinic. With the pressure of No. 77 lifted, he dominated the ice and the scoreboard. He got No. 78 at 18:16 and, for good measure, made it 6-3 with his 79th goal just 17 seconds from the final buzzer, both on slapshots.

It was Gretzky's eighth hat trick of the season, including the three four-goal games and the one five-goal outburst. For the fourth straight game, he'd scored five points. And, single-handedly, he'd won another game for the Oilers.

Following these heroics, Gretzky was shuttled to an interview room that overflowed with print, TV and radio reporters, cameramen and NHL officials. The first order of business was the reading of a congratulatory message from President Reagan.

"Congratulations on your extraordinary achievement," Reagan's wire said. "The record for most goals in a season is one that many people thought would never be broken. Your brief National Hockey League career has already produced many record-breaking performances. But I know that this record is of special significance."

Of all the press conferences Wayne was subjected to in his special season, he seemed to enjoy this one the most. The first thing he did was turn to Esposito and thank Phil for "following me around."

"I don't think I was nervous," he said. "The only thing I felt was that Phil was kind enough to be here. I wanted to do it so Phil could get back to whatever he had to do."

Gretzky said he never despaired of reaching No. 77 in Buffalo. "I never feel a game is over until 60 minutes are played," he said. "You can score with one second left. So I never say I can't score."

He thanked the Buffalo fans—and every other hockey fan—for their support.

"Everywhere, in every NHL arena, the fans have been tremendous," he

Oiler Wayne Gretzky shoots the puck past Sabre goalie Don Edwards to score his record breaking 77th goal during 3rd period play here 2/24/1982.

Wayne Gretzky (99) is hugged by his teammates in a fall together on the ice. He had just scored his 77th goal of the season breaking Phil Esposito's single season goal scoring record of 76. ➤

JOFA
KOHO

KOHO
KOHO
JOFA

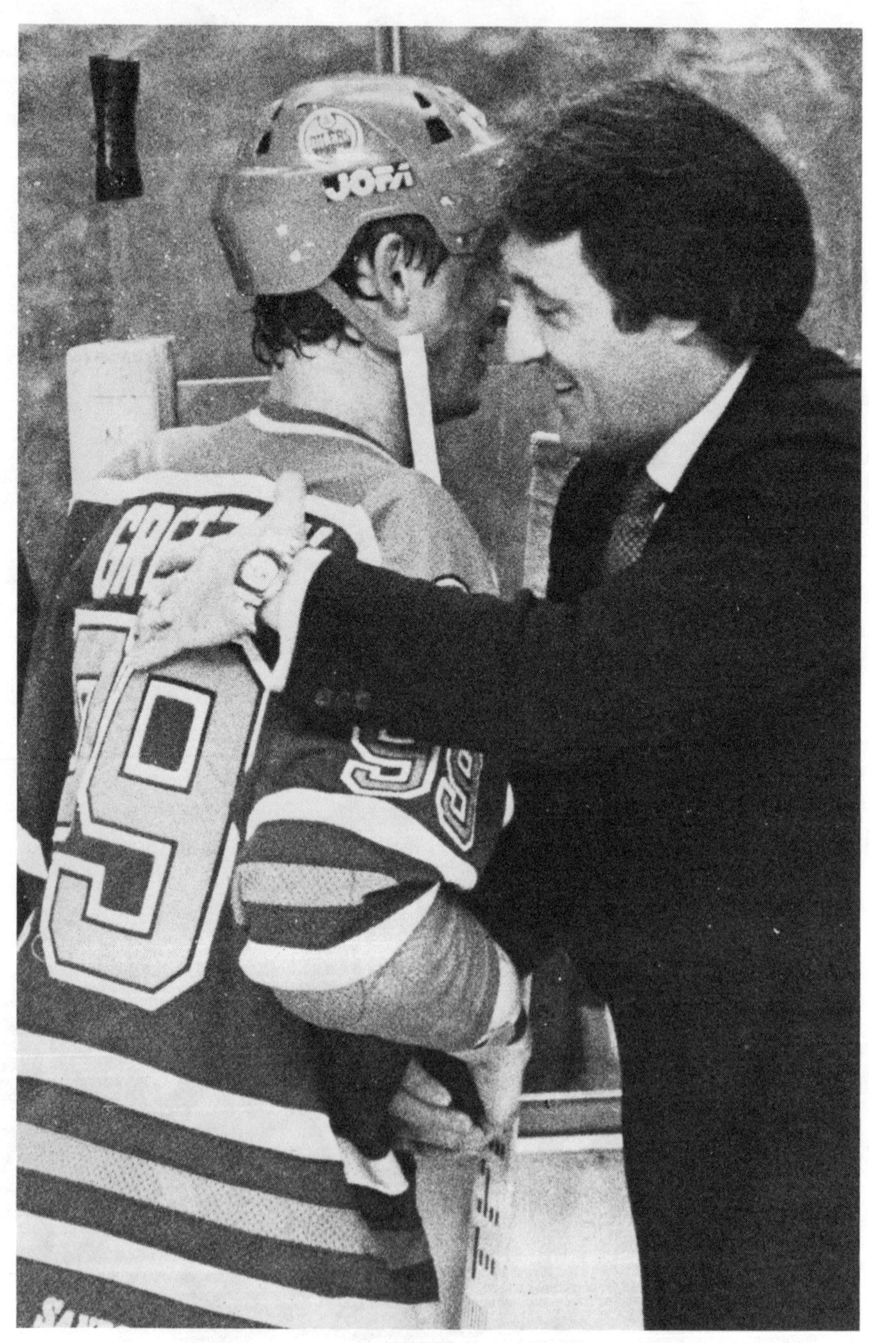

Phil Esposito gives Wayne a pat on the back.

The puck Wayne used to score his record breaking 77th goal.

said. "They were kind to me in Pittsburgh last year (when he set the single-season points mark), in Detroit and here tonight. They've been great everywhere."

Then, as he always does, he spread around the credit.

"I would like to see some recognition for my teammates," he said. "No player can do it alone. This is a team which has grown together, gotten better together.

"I feel very fortunate to have accomplished so much so early in my career," he said. "I'm playing in an era that suits my style best. When I broke in at 18 or 19, I listened to the older guys who had been around. That's helped me."

As expected, praise flowed from all quarters for the Great Gretzky. Pocklington called him the "Nureyev of sports, the superstar's superstar. He'll keep breaking records and setting the standards for excellence for years. He's doing great things for the Oilers, the NHL and hockey. For Wayne, the sky's the limit. If he stays healthy, he could average 100 goals and 125 assists a season."

Pocklington then gave what might be the perfect description of Wayne Gretzky, the ice hockey scoring machine.

"He has such vitality and a creativity that never stops," the Oilers' owner said. "He picks the right plays for the right situations. He has an uncanny ability to slow down the game so that it is being played in slow motion in his mind. But he's going full speed. He holds the puck for seconds and it seems like minutes are going by. A guy just runs out of words trying to describe Wayne."

Esposito, who never runs out of words, spilled a couple hundred on the subject of Gretzky, Orr and, yes, Phil Esposito.

"I remember a few years ago my Dad calling me and saying he'd seen a kid play in Sault Ste. Marie who was going to break all of my records," Espo recalled. "I said, 'Oh yeah, what's his name?'

" 'Wayne Gretzky,' my father said. I said, 'Great.'

"My Dad called me from Florida today and asked me when Wayne was going to do it. I said I hoped tonight because I was tired of following him around.

"The publicity Wayne has brought to the league has been tremendous. It really helps hockey out because it creates the image of great hockey players, not idiots.

"In my opinion, he has the greatest amount of talent in the league. He has total intensity and a desire that outweighs anybody else. That, plus all that God-given talent, is what makes him so great.

"I can't compare him with Bobby—you don't compare human beings," said Esposito. "Orr had as much talent as anyone I've ever seen. But I don't think Bobby could have scored as much as Wayne."

Orr's career was cut short by injuries that gave him knees which would shame an old lady. Does Gretzky face the possibility of an early burnout, with still more worlds to conquer and records to establish that might last forever?

"I've been playing like this and this much since I was 6," said Gretzky, who thinks he has goofed off when he hasn't been on the ice for 30 minutes (most top-calibre forwards average 20-22 minutes a game). "Back then, people said I'd be washed up by 12.

"I'm sure it will catch up with me. But I'm not worrying about it."

Game 65, vs. Penguins at Pittsburgh

The sporting world had a couple of days to ponder the magnitude of Gretzky's achievement in Buffalo. Gretzky had a couple of days to sit back and enjoy the praise being heaped upon him from the avid hockey following and those just becoming interested in the game because of him.

The Oilers, basking in the glow for supporting Gretzky on the way to his remarkable season, were able to relax, knowing they now could concentrate on the rest of the schedule without much emphasis on Wayne's statistics.

The third stop on the extended road trip was Pittsburgh, where Gretzky surpassed Esposito's points record the previous season. A full house and local television coverage were some of the benefits the Penguins derived as Edmonton made its only visit to the Igloo.

The Penguins were an injured bunch as they faced the red-hot Oilers, who hadn't lost in almost four weeks. Most damaging, the two players usually assigned to shadow Gretzky, Gregg Sheppard and Mark Johnson, were among the wounded Penguins.

"We'll use George Ferguson and Andre St. Laurent against him," said Penguins coach Ed Johnston. "Gretzky can be stopped. Kasper always gives him a rough time and Shepp and Mark have done a good job against him for us. All it takes is hard work, concentration and sacrifice."

St. Laurent, just up from the minors, had never been assigned to check Gretzky. He did, however, have a plan.

"I haven't really been told to check one guy for a game," said St. Laurent, who'd seen duty with the Islanders, Red Wings and Kings before being picked up on waivers from LA. "I've mostly checked a whole line with other defensive players playing with me as a unit.

"I don't know how the coach wants to work it. If he wants me to stick close to Gretzky, I'm gonna put a little stickum on the hands and have them get a rope and tie me to him."

Though St. Laurent didn't get to use his rope trick on Gretzky, he did an effective job. Gretzky was held without a goal for 59 minutes in the wide-open contest in which a total of 83 shots were fired at the two goalies.

Hunter's slapshot eluded Penguins goalie Michel Dion after hitting a defenseman's stick early in the game and Anderson made it 2-0 midway through the opening period. With the Oilers holding a two-man advantage, Gretzky fed Coffey at the point and his hard slapshot was tapped home by Anderson.

Low's goaltending kept the Penguins quiet until only 3½ minutes remained. Ferguson made a pair of sharp moves to fake out Fogolin and Low before putting the puck over the prone goalie.

The 16,033 fans in the Igloo finally had something to raise their voices about. For the next two minutes, they exercised their vocal cords with vigor. But, as he'd been doing all year, Gretzky silenced the hostile mob with an empty-net goal, firing the puck 100 feet into the unguarded cage after Dion had been lifted for an extra skater.

Lowe added another empty-netter with just three seconds left for a 4-1 Edmonton triumph.

"I thought we did a pretty good job on Gretzky," said Johnston. "But he still got more points than we did."

Even the Soviets call him The Great Gretzky.

Game 66, vs. Capitals at Washington

When Subaru, the automobile company, comes out with its next model, don't be surprised if it's called the Gretzky.

Subaru sponsors the NHL Player of the Week, Month and Year awards. Gretzky specializes in winning them.

The February award was the fifth in a row this season for Gretzky. He also won the monthly honors in April 1981 and was named Subaru's Player of the Year for the 1980-81 season. He would have no competition in repeating this year.

No other NHL player had ever won more than one monthly award but this marked the seventh for the Edmonton ace.

Such awards should come as no shock to anyone by now, least of all Gretzky. In October, Gretzky had 13 goals and 27 points in 13 games to earn monthly honors even though he was not named Player of the Week during the month.

In November, he notched 18 goals and 37 points in 13 games and was the weekly award winner once.

For December, when he leaped past the 50-goal plateau, Wayne had 19 goals and 44 points in 14 contests, scoring in all but the final game of the month. Twice he was selected Player of the Week and he shared that distinction once.

January saw Gretzky continue his incredible scoring pace with 17 goals and 38 points, scoring in all but one of Edmonton's 15 games. He won the weekly award twice in January.

Gretzky culminated his amazing string of monthly honors with a 15-goal, 35 point February, in which he played in only 11 games. As if to place an exclamation point on the month, Gretzky had two goals and an assist against Washington as the Oilers skated to their second straight 4-1 win. They were 9-1-1 for the month.

During February, Gretzky scored a point in all 11 games, the highlights, of course, being four consecutive five-point nights and the record-setter in Buffalo. Gretzky was Player of the Week twice, though he shared it one week.

The last time the Oilers visited Washington, Gretzky raced from the gate, getting a goal and two assists in the first 10 minutes. Then he was blanked the rest of the way and the Caps rallied for a 6-6 tie.

This time, Gretzky was right where he was supposed to be down the stretch—on the ice, scoring and setting up goals.

The Caps, sparked by a sellout crowd of 18,130, went ahead on an early second-period, power-play goal by Gustafsson. But Gretzky got his 81st to knot it 1:40 later. In the third period, after Messier broke the tie, Gretzky spotted Kurri and fed him for a shorthanded goal, then put the game on ice with his second goal of the night as Kurri returned the assist with 40 seconds to play.

It was a fitting way to end the usually dreary month of February, a four-week period during which the sports world focused on hockey for a change.

The NHL had Gretzky to thank for that.

Game 67, vs. Canadiens at Montreal

The next stop for the Wayne Gretzky Traveling Magic Show was Montreal. If any team could halt the Oilers' unbeaten streak, now at 10, and Gretzky's consecutive game points streak, now at 22, six shy of Guy Lafleur's league mark, Les Canadiens seemed like the right candidates to turn the trick.

Montreal was far and away the best defensive team in the NHL. In this season of stratospheric scores and unchallenged attacks, the stingy Canadiens were surrendering fewer than three goals a game. Nobody else was close.

The Oilers had a loss and a tie in previous meetings this season with Les Habitants, whom they sent reeling in the '81 playoffs with that opening-round sweep. At that time, Gretzky was viewed as if he was royalty by the denizens of Montreal, who felt Wayne had singlehandedly laid the Canadiens to waste.

The Montreal players had no intention of treating Gretzky like a king. But their thoughts were occupied by the kid known in French quarters as "Le Grande Gretzky."

Many Canadiens explained that their defensive corps would play the vital role in slowing down the Oiler Express, engineered by No. 99.

"The defensemen have a lot more to do with trying to check Gretzky than with other players in the league, even great ones like Bryan Trottier," offered Montreal defenseman Brian Engblom. "The thing with Gretzky is that he sees everything in front of him. He's not looking at the puck so he knows what's happening at all times. He burns a lot of people that way, especially those who run at him.

"What you don't do against someone like Gretzky is take a run at him," added Engblom, one of the NHL's steadiest defensemen and second in the plus-minus ratings (showing the number of times a player is on-ice for goals scored by and against his club with the teams at even strength) to Gretzky.

"He'll get around you . . . somehow. I've always wondered why Gretzky doesn't get hit more. Why doesn't he take as much abuse as Guy Lafleur has taken over the years? He's pretty hard to catch against the boards, though, and you wouldn't want to take him on at mid-ice because he'll leave you looking like a fool."

Bob Gainey, the league's premier checker for a half-decade, rarely looks like a fool on the ice. But he knows that Gretzky can turn anybody inside-out.

"With Gretzky, there are always surprises," said Gainey. "He'll start down one side and end up on the other. He's always around the net. He'll draw defensemen to him but the danger is that you can't have two defensemen going after him if he's got a stride or two on the guys checking him. Then you get into trouble with the other forwards on the Oilers, and they've got plenty of them.

"With some players, we can put a center or a left wing or a right wing on him and the job is done. But Gretzky demands more attention than that from everyone on the ice. The forwards and the defensemen are responsible because there's no one guy who can stop him."

The guys usually handed the chore of becoming Gretzky's alter ego for Montreal are centers Doug Jarvis and Doug Risebrough. This two-headed Doug excels on defense, is superb on faceoffs (especially Jarvis), intense (Risebrough) and sometimes chippy.

"It's more than a one-man job," said Jarvis. "Sometimes, it's like a six-man job, from the goalie on out. He's always breaking out of his zone and the puck always seems to get to his stick. If he does have a couple of strides on you, the defensemen have to take him. They'll find him in their area a lot more often than any other player in the league.

"Trottier plays a very physical game but he also does a lot of checking. So it's not as hard to follow him around. Gretzky is more difficult because he's all over the place and in control of what he's doing all the time."

Montreal controlled matters in the opening 20 minutes of the game but was deadlocked 2-2 at the first intermission. Gretzky assisted on Coffey's power-play tally halfway through the session.

Wayne collected another assist in the second period when Anderson beat Wamsley in the Montreal goal. That tied it 3-3 and the game ended that way, though the Oilers fired 16 shots at the rookie goalie in the third period.

"Wamsley was real hot," said Gretzky. "I think he got them the point. We played well enough to win."

The Canadiens' largest crowd of the season to this point—they would draw 74 more fans for a game with Quebec in the final week of the campaign —had been treated to an entertaining though not enchanting evening. Gretzky's two assists did not constitute anything "kingly," but he had left few of the 18,101 fans disappointed.

The tie would be followed by six straight wins for Montreal. For Edmonton, the season's bleakest hours were about to hit.

Game 68, vs. Nordiques at Quebec

Alain Cote won't ever get into the NHL records for his scoring touch because he barely has one. Cote makes his living, quite simply, by trying to handcuff those players who do have the touch. Gretzky has enough scoring skills to keep 100 Alain Cotes busy.

On this night, Cote does his work splendidly. He's been Gretzky's constant companion on ice and, although Wayne picks up two assists, Cote holds him without a shot on goal. It is the first time since October 27 against the Islanders—the night Gretzky was slashed by Smith—that he's been held shotless.

Not surprisingly, the Oilers lose to Quebec 6-4. Again, not surprisingly, Cote is the center of attraction after the game.

"There are two ways to play against Gretzky," said Nordiques coach Michel Bergeron. "I've played an offensive line against him in order to make him play not only offensively but also make him think of his defensive role in the game. But that can work the opposite way because, if he has the puck most of the time, your best offensive players don't have it, so you've thrown off your attack.

"The other thing to do is to play your two best checking players against him. One guy can't do it all game because Gretzky plays too many minutes. If you have two guys, you use them on Gretzky by alternating them."

Quebec, however, does not have two Cotes. The Nordiques are lucky to have one because Cote is about the only skater on their roster who gladly sacrifices offense.

Quebec and Edmonton had met twice earlier in the season, with Bergeron most often employing his former method of defense against Gretzky. The results: an 11-4 Quebec loss in which Wayne had four goals, and a 9-8 Nordiques' victory in which Gretzky easily could have had another four with some luck.

For this final matchup of two of the most explosive teams in hockey, Bergeron was set to put Cote on Gretzky, moving the four-year veteran from his normal left wing spot into the middle to joust with Gretzky.

One mistake the Nordiques made came 7:25 into the second period, when they allowed Wayne to establish position behind the Quebec net. He fed the puck out front to Messier, who got it to Lumley for Edmonton's first goal. Ironically, Messier also would be held shotless in the game, meaning the Nordiques had shackled the Oilers' top two scorers.

In the third period, Gretzky hit Siltanen with a pass and the defenseman from Finland rifled the puck past Quebec goalie Daniel Bouchard to tie the score 4-4. The Oilers had blown a 3-1 margin but rallied.

The rally was wasted when Peter Stastny, in the midst of his own magnificent season, and Real Cloutier put the puck past Low to give Quebec the victory.

Cote was asked if he was nervous before the game.

"Facing Gretzky, who would not be nervous a little?" he replied. "When the game starts, though, you forget it because you're concentrating only on your job. Against Gretzky, you must concentrate extra hard."

Apparently, Cote's concentration was perfect. Gretzky didn't have even one good scoring chance for one of the few times in his life. Cote wasn't on him all the way as Wayne skated his normal double shift. But Cote did cast an awfully long, effective shadow when he attached himself to No. 99.

"You must deny him the chance to get started when he has the puck," said Cote. "The best way is to deny him the puck. I'm proud he didn't get a shot on goal because he has 82 (goals) already, which means not too many times has he been held without one (shot).

"Still, he fooled me on those two assists, which showed you that you can't let up one second on him."

It was Edmonton's fourth game in five nights and the sixth on the grueling eight-game, 17-day road trip that had begun so magnificently in Detroit and Buffalo. The loss snapped the Oilers' 11-game unbeaten streak, during which Gretzky closed in on and then passed the points and goals records, but they'd played their best hockey of the season throughout the streak. Now would come their worst.

"We were a tired team tonight," admitted Sather. "The game against Montreal last night took a lot out of us and the Nordiques are a good team that caught us a little flat."

Whatever life the Oilers had left was squelched by a left wing with no scoring touch playing at center and stymying Gretzky.

Game 69
vs. Rockies at Colorado

With Lafleur's record-scoring streak dead in his sights, Gretzky drew a blank in, can you believe it?, Denver. The Rockies, a financially struggling franchise and the worst on-ice team in the NHL, moved mountains into Gretzky's way all night and came away with a 5-2 upset of the Oilers.

By failing to get a point, Gretzky's longest consecutive game points streak of his career ended at 24, just four short of Lafleur's mark, set in 1976-77. Like the rest of his teammates, Gretzky was lethargic. The long trip, which would conclude in Los Angeles in four days, was taking its toll on the team.

"You wouldn't know the Rockies are a last-place team and having so much trouble getting people to the games," said Sather. "Tonight was their night, not ours."

A sellout crowd turned out at McNichols Arena to see what the Great Gretzky was all about. In two trips to Denver this season, the Oilers had drawn a total of 15,451 people. Those games, on October 24 and December 16, came well before Gretzky had set any records.

But this time, a full house of 16,384 was in attendance and the Oilers didn't give them a very good show. The Rockies took charge early and never allowed Wayne to break free. Of course, Gretzky, in one of his worst performances of the year, might not have done anything against Rockies goalie Chico Resch even if he managed some decent scoring opportunities.

Resch, having possibly the best season of his eight-year career—it must be remembered that most of the first seven seasons were spent with the talent-rich Islanders, where he got loads of help—is a fine assessor of hockey skills.

He is also the NHL's resident motor mouth, the man who once said, "If I wasn't talking, I wouldn't know what to say." He had plenty to say about the Gretzky phenomenon.

"Here's this frail-looking kid who doesn't seem to be doing anything special," said Resch. "It's not like Bobby Orr, where you'd marvel at him going end to end with the puck—which he seemed to do all the time. Wayne's just doing things and setting records no one dreamed could be accomplished. And you can't really pinpoint why.

"What you have to understand is that people will always attempt to criticize or rationalize what they can't explain," added Resch.

Resch believes that, with the incredible amount of publicity Gretzky has received all season, there would have to be some detractors. According to the ebullient goaltender, Gretzky was somewhat victimized by an underlying prejudice against the WHA harbored by oldtimers and hard-liners from the NHL establishment.

"He's from the WHA, which a lot of old-time NHL people still don't accept," said Resch. "And a lot of people criticizing Gretzky are the same ones who said he wouldn't make it in the tougher league. When someone just comes in and tears things apart, people have got to search for negatives."

A comparison with what Roger Maris went through in 1961 as he chased Babe Ruth's single season home run record of 60, seems apt. As the pressure built during Maris' chase, detractors surfaced from everywhere. Baseball purists were incensed that anyone would challenge the one and only Babe's most hallowed achievement.

After Maris broke the record in the 162nd game of the season—Ruth had only 154 games in 1927—his name was accompanied by an asterisk in the record books, forever placing his feat in a secondary position to the Babe's. That asterisk was more a question mark than anything.

Maris was a changed man after surpassing the Babe in 1961. He went from a decent interview to a bitter non-interview and his life and career were troubled until premature retirement.

Will Wayne Gretzky turn cold and unavailable, even hostile to the press just because some observers have seen fit to belittle his accomplishments? That's about as likely as Resch taking a vow of silence.

"Look, they can say all they want about Wayne," said Resch. "They can say he doesn't like to play defense or he's a lazy checker or he can't take a hit or that he wouldn't have made it in a six-team league.

"Gretzky would have made it in a one-team league."

Game 70, vs. Kings at Los Angeles

"Thank goodness that's over."

The end of the prolonged road trip was about the only thing that could make Messier, who uttered the statement above, and his teammates smile. The journey that had begun so positively with four victories ended miserably.

"I guess when you go 4-3-1 on a road trip," Messier added after a 3-2 loss to the Kings, "you shouldn't be too down. But it was awful long and we did lose the last three."

For the first time all season, the Oilers lost three in a row. And they were beaten by Quebec, a decent team, and Colorado and Los Angeles, two of the NHL's more humble contingents. No defeats at the hands of the Islanders or Canadiens, which can be easily explained.

Gretzky had two assists as the Oilers rallied from 0-3 in the third period but fell short.

"I've been getting good opportunities until the last game and tonight," he said. "In these two games, I've been shut down pretty good."

He knew why.

"We had to be a little weary tonight," he said, mentioning the eight-game itinerary which took the Oilers from Edmonton to Detroit, Buffalo, Pittsburgh, Washington, Montreal, Quebec City, Denver and LA. "We're paid good money to play but being on the road for almost three weeks is ridiculous. We all have families and wives and whether you're a doctor of whatever, you miss them if you're gone that long."

As had become the custom on the road trip, Gretzky was shuttled to a separate press conference. For the first time, he displayed a bit of annoyance at it all. But still he showed and answered whatever questions were hurled at him.

"I'm getting accustomed to separate press conferences," he admitted, "but sometimes it's a little embarrassing when others have had good games and I'm alone with the press."

If anyone deserved his own press conference this night, it was Kings center Dan Bonar, who had put the clamps to Gretzky for most of the game; Wayne's two assists came with Bonar on the bench.

"You can't say enough about Dan Bonar," said Kings coach Don Perry. "He shut out Gretzky tonight. Gretzky gets so much ice time and the job Bonar did on him shows the stamina and strength he has."

Bonar was the first LA checker to have any luck against Gretzky all season. A 25-year-old second-year player, Bonar's chief means of remaining in the NHL will always be as a defensive forward—he would wind up with 13 goals in 1981-82, two more than in his rookie year.

"He's so hard to stay with because his anticipation and knowledge of the game are so great," said Bonar. "You have to almost forget there's anyone else on the ice when you guard him. You try to be right on top of him wherever he goes whenever he's on the ice. Of course, that's half the game or more.

"It was nice to shut Wayne down. He knows what to do and where to be every minute he plays and he usually knows how to get away from checkers."

Not this time, though Gretzky played much better than in Colorado the previous contest.

"We're not playing like we were in the first half of the year," he said. "We're going to have to get back to fundamentals.

"I guess a slump is a little understandable when you get this late in the season and haven't really had one," he noted. "When we get home tomorrow, it should get easier for us.

"We've been away a long time."

Three games too long, for sure.

Game 71, vs. Sabres at Edmonton

The Oilers carried their first three-game losing slide of the season into the matchup with the Sabres. Buffalo carried a grudge.

Most especially, Don Edwards was out for some revenge. It was Edwards, of course, who had been beaten in Buffalo for the record-setting 77th goal—and Nos. 78 and 79 to boot—16 days earlier.

Edwards had been a busy man, with a string of 22 straight starts dating back to mid-January. Few of those appearances meant so much to him.

"Sure I had it on my mind before the game," Edwards said of the night Gretzky passed Esposito at Edwards' expense. "I wanted to stop him. But I also wanted to win the game and not get caught up thinking about Gretzky."

He didn't. Edwards played "as well as any goalie we've faced this year," according to Sather. He made 42 saves, some of them near-miraculous, and the Sabres won 3-2. Gretzky didn't have a point, though he felt he should have. And the Oilers should have had a tie.

Edwards foiled Gretzky on a breakaway with 6:01 left, but the puck slithered behind him and Hughes knocked it home. Referee Kerry Fraser ruled no goal, saying he'd lost sight of the puck.

Momentarily, Gretzky lost sight of his senses. He had to be restrained from going after Fraser. Remember, this was the same Wayne Gretzky who won the Lady Byng Trophy for his gentlemanly play. But he was so mad he was prepared to charge the rookie ref.

"It should have been a goal," Gretzky claimed. "I think it took a little bit out of us. We were upset at what happened but it's no excuse. I think we had ample time to put them away and we didn't."

After he'd cooled down, Gretzky couldn't bring himself to blast Fraser.

"The ref is doing the best he can," he said. "That's the thing you always have to remember. In the heat of the action you get a little bit excited, a little

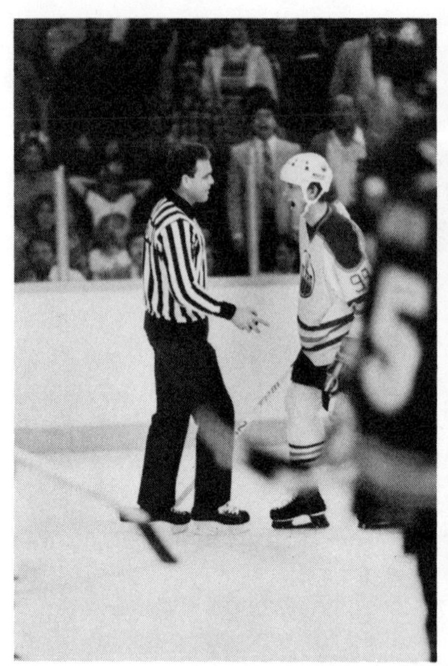

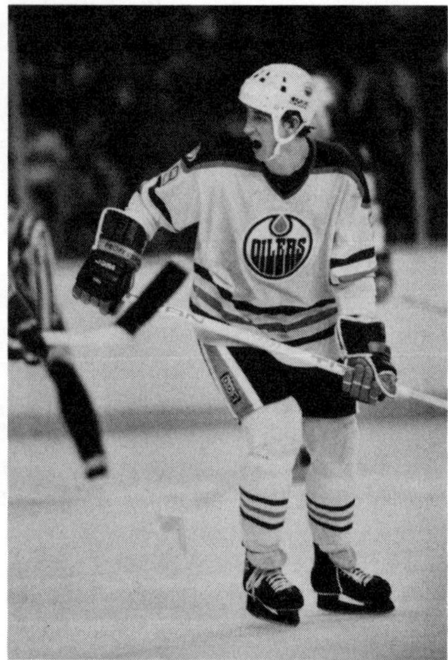

An enraged Gretzky argues call by referee Kerry Fraser which disallows game-tying goal.

bit frustrated. I don't think I would have gone at him but I was mad. It was a big goal to lose, especially the way we lost it."

Fraser, showing the kind of candor most sports officials could use a dose of, admitted to his error.

"We all make mistakes," he said. "But I think when you make them you have to admit them. In that situation, I perhaps could have been in a better position. Had I been in a different position, I would have seen the puck fall behind him."

The loss put the Oilers in a tough position. With only nine games left, they now trailed the Islanders by six points in the overall points race, something they desperately wanted to win.

"That," said Gretzky, "makes it even worse."

Game 72, vs. Canucks at Edmonton

Things began to get better and would continue to improve through the end of the regular season. The Oilers ended their longest losing streak of the campaign at four games by downing Vancouver 5-3 as Gretzky registered three assists. Edmonton didn't play all that well but skated off with two points as Fuhr contributed his best game in several weeks, making 36 saves.

"When you are outshot 39-23 and still win, you have to credit the goal-tending," said Sather. "We may have lost a little zip but we'll get that back."

Gretzky failed to score for the sixth straight game and fell off the 100-goal pace. He was more concerned about the team's performances, however.

"We all knew we'd snap out of it but you begin to wonder what can go wrong next," he said of the losing streak. "The road trip took a lot out of us. Then, we lost the first game at home against Buffalo and we were down even more.

"This win has to help."

Game 73, vs. Kings at Edmonton

A sweating Gretzky sat beneath the blazing lights of the television studio. It was between the first and second periods of the game with the Kings, the same Kings who embarrassed themselves by giving up four goals twice to Gretzky earlier in the season. These Kings also had gotten some redemption by blanking the Oilers' super center a few nights earlier.

The Kings were having a schizophrenic season. For most of the campaign, they were the worst defensive team in hockey. But now the Kings were hot. They had plugged the sieve they called a defense, registered two shutouts in their last three games and were straightening out their act as the playoffs—and a matchup with the Oilers—drew near.

Gretzky, too, was showing schizo tendencies. He had gone six straight games without hitting the net. He had 82 goals in his hip pocket but the fact that he had temporarily lost the touch was weighing on his mind.

Now, after missing a wide-open net on a first-period power play and being robbed by Kings goalie Mario Lessard on another attempt, Gretzky was spending his between-periods respite doing yet another TV interview.

The game was being televised throughout the States on the USA cable network. It was billed "The Wayne Gretzky Show," so, naturally, Gretzky was to be at center stage, on and off the ice.

The interview, conducted by USA's Al Trautwig, was one of the better sessions Gretzky had to endure during his skate to glory. He joked with Trautwig about the line of Western-style clothes carrying his name and admitted to being a virtual stranger to his Western wear ship in Edmonton.

"I don't shop there too often," Gretzky told Trautwig. "The clothes are too expensive for me."

Wayne described how he relaxes away from the arena and he spoke of his role as an athlete, an Oiler and a hockey player who, as he fully realized, was carrying much of the sport's credibility on his back.

"If what I'm doing is good for hockey and if I can help hockey, it makes me happy," he said. "I'm paid to help the team win and that's my purpose with the Oilers. I'm paid to score goals and if my scoring goals gets us more wins, then I'm doing my job."

"If you were interviewing Wayne Gretzky," Trautwig asked, "what question would you ask?"

"Can I still score goals?" Gretzky replied.

A little while later, Wayne had answered his own query—twice.

Los Angeles had built a 2-0 lead on a pair of goals by Dionne. Prior to the game, Sather said his strategy for stopping Dionne was simple: he would place Gretzky opposite the slick Kings' center.

"The best way to stop Dionne is not to let him have the puck," reasoned Sather. "Wayne has the puck all the time."

Sather also wanted to rid Gretzky of the shadow of Bonar, who has stymied him in LA.

But Sather's strategy backfired as Dionne outplayed Gretzky for 25 minutes and twice beat Fuhr.

The Kings kept charging right at the Oilers, even with a 2-0 lead on the road, which would seem an ideal time to turn conservative. They were doing a pretty fair job of shackling Gretzky as well, and the SRO crowd at the Coliseum sensed it. A few more minutes without a Gretzky explosion might have been enough for the fans to ask, "Can he still score goals?"

Some excellent work by Kurri kept the play in the LA zone with barely more than four minutes remaining in the second stanza. The puck came to Gretzky to the left of Lessard at the bottom of the faceoff circle. Gretzky made an attempt to skate around a pair of Kings but was hooked just enough to lose his balance.

Still, he got off a wrist shot, which was blocked by the defense as Gretzky fell to the ice. As he lay almost flat on his belly, Gretzky took another swipe at the puck. Lessard never saw it whiz past.

No. 83.

"That was a long time in coming," Gretzky said after the game.

"You score a lot of goals, then go so long without one, it feels strange. You feel like you're letting the team down, especially when you're not scoring and the team's losing. It was a good goal to get."

It wasn't the only one he'd get this night.

A bit later in the period, Hughes was penalized and Sather sent Gretzky out to kill the two minutes. Shorthanded situations would be one of the best times for the Oilers to rest Gretzky, to cut down on his inordinate playing time. But Sather said throughout the season that a) he never thought of doing it and b) Gretzky is such an overpowering force on the ice that his mere presence can disrupt an opponent's power play.

It did exactly that against the Kings. While LA was deep in concentration on the power play, looking to pull ahead by two goals again, Kurri and Gretzky were springing a trap.

When Kurri and Gretzky kill penalties together, their minds are not 100 percent preoccupied with defense. Any slight opening—and who creates openings and takes advantage of even the minutest ones better than Gretzky?—is an invitation.

Their thoughts thus bound, both Gretzky and Kurri spotted that opening and Wayne snuck into center ice just as Kurri took hold of the puck in his defensive zone. Kurri didn't need to search for his penalty-killing partner. He knew exactly where Wayne would be.

Kurri hit a now-breaking Gretzky with a perfect pass. In full stride, Gretzky skated unmolested towards Lessard.

The sight of Wayne Gretzky bearing down on you, puck in his possession and nobody around to help is one a goalie might compare with what a swimmer must feel standing on a deserted beach just before he must swim across a body of water. And this body of water is the ocean.

As the tidal wave with No. 99 on his white jersey headed straight at Lessard, the goalie made a quick move out of the net. He waited for Gretzky to make his move.

"You have to challenge him to do something," said Lessard, who played a terrific game. "Hopefully, that something is just what you wanted him to do."

Gretzky made enough of a fake to get Lessard to commit himself. Then Gretzky shifted the puck to his backhand and popped it home, with Lessard sprawled in front of the net, thoroughly beaten.

No. 84. Yes, Wayne, you can still score goals.

Game 74, vs. Penguins at Edmonton

Considering the pace at which he'd been destroying so many NHL clubs, Gretzky's numbers against the Penguins weren't particularly overwhelming. In two meetings, both Edmonton wins, Wayne had two goals and two assists.

He surpassed that in this game, a 10-4 bombing of Pittsburgh in which Edmonton raced to 3-0 and 6-1 margins.

"The past few games, we played better defensively than we had all season," said Gretzky, who had his 10th hat trick of the year for yet another NHL record, plus two assists. "But our record wasn't that good (1-4-2 in the last seven outings).

"So before the game we said, 'Let's go ahead and score eight or nine goals.' If we weren't concentrating on our offense, who knows what might've happened."

What did happen was Gretzky's setting that record for three-goal games in a season, breaking the mark of nine set by Mike Bossy last season. He also set up Kurri's 30th goal of the year to give him a record 110 assists, eclipsing his 109 of the 1980-81 campaign. And the three goals gave Gretzky 87, which smashed another Bossy mark: the Islander right wing had 68 regular-season goals and 17 in the playoffs for 85 last season.

"You have to play disciplined against a guy who can freewheel the way he can," said Penguins coach Ed Johnston. "We let Gretzky do what he does best, which is everything."

Indeed. He set up Lariviere's first goal of the season as well as Kurri's score. And he beat Dion once in each period.

"You just have to forget about a game like that," said Dion, who took no solace from the fact that Gretzky had done precisely the same to nearly every other goalie in the NHL. "There's nothing you can do about it. He was too good for us tonight and so were they."

Gretzky's first goal was an example of what makes him so special. It came after he made a careless mistake and it showed the kind of fierce determination which sets great players apart from mere mortals.

With Edmonton holding a two-man edge, Hagman broke into the Pittsburgh zone and found Gretzky alone at the right point. With no one to impede his progress to the net, Gretzky's 85th goal seemed seconds away.

But he blew the pass, letting it trickle off his stick and out over the blue line.

"Some players would get so frustrated at missing a chance like that they'd lose their effectiveness," said Sather.

Gretzky turned around, recaptured his poise after slamming his stick on the ice, and picked up the puck. He headed directly down the right side at full speed, cut across the middle as the Pittsburgh defense backed in, and fired a shot past a screened Dion.

In a matter of seconds, Gretzky had blown a certain goal, turned around and started over again until he did it right.

The Penguins marveled at the show Gretzky had put on, at the way he willed his team to victory by quickly erasing an error and scoring a significant goal. The Penguins were never in the game after Gretzky made it 2-0.

"Great players do things like that all the time," said Johnston. "It shouldn't surprise us, I guess, when Gretzky is able to come up with efforts like that. That's what sets him apart. That's why he's able to do so much."

Gretzky wasn't so sure he was getting his due from hockey observers. He told *Pittsburgh Press* columnist Pete Wevurski that "it seems the more I do, the more fault some people find with me.

"The more goals and points I get, the more I hear things like, 'But he can't play defense,'" Gretzky said. "Or, 'But to be really great, he's got to keep doing it for 10 years from now.'

"Or, 'He'd be just another player in the six-team era.'

"I seem to be caught in circumstances I'd rather not be caught in," he added. "I'm always being compared to Bobby Orr, Gordie Howe, Rocket Richard and Howie Morenz.

"You can't really do that, though. Every 10 years, it (the game) changes. Maybe 20 years ago, I couldn't play my style. I'm fortunate to be playing in an era that's best suited to my style.

"The thing about a professional athlete is that you're going to have some people behind you 100 percent all the way, and other people who don't favor you or who had other favorites, so they never give you credit.

"I don't know, I guess the worst thing of all is accomplishment."

Game 75, vs. Flames at Edmonton

Several milestones were within Gretzky's reach on this night but only one came his way.

Gretzky entered the game with 197 points. 200 was staring him and the Edmonton fans in the face. But, just as happened in pursuit of Esposito's goals record, Gretzky would fall just short of the 200-point mark at home and would have to reach it on the road.

But he did achieve another important figure as he scored his 500th career point in only his 234th NHL game (that figure does not include his 110 points in the WHA).

"The goal was more important because it got us a tie, not because of 500 points," said Gretzky, who tied the game with 6:56 remaining and only 23 seconds after he fed Messier for a breakaway that lifted the Oilers within 3-2.

The Flames, playing without Paul Reinhart, Jim Peplinski and Phil Russell, three of their top players, established a 3-1 lead before Messier got No. 45 and Gretzky put in his 88th.

"I don't know where Gretzky came from," said Flames goalie Rejean Lemelin, speaking of the tying goal. "I was playing the shot by Anderson and then there he was and then there the puck was, in the net."

Gretzky would be stuck at 199 for nearly a week as, by a strange quirk in the schedule, the Oilers would have six days between games.

"Gretz and I were driving to the rink and talking about it today," said Lowe. "We're going to use the time off to prepare for the playoffs.

"It's a whole new ballgame now . . . fierce competition, nice weather. We imagined ourselves in the Stanley Cup finals."

Imagining was all they would do when it came to the finals. But, for now, Gretzky's pursuit of 200 was making the headlines.

Reaching 200 on the road didn't bother him much.

"I wish the fans at home could have seen it but getting 200 at home or on the road doesn't matter," he said. "I realize that by going on the road and playing in front of sellout crowds, that if, after they watch me play, there are still some people who wonder if I'm any good, then I must not be doing my job."

The 500th point of his NHL career.

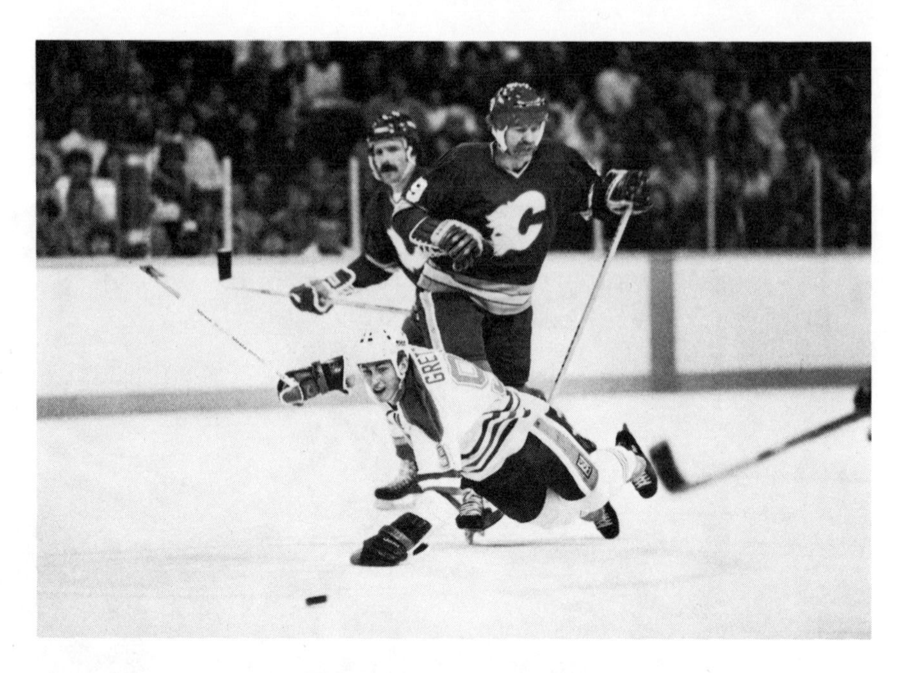

For Gretzky, a rough landing. For Lanny McDonald of the Flames, a two minute penalty.

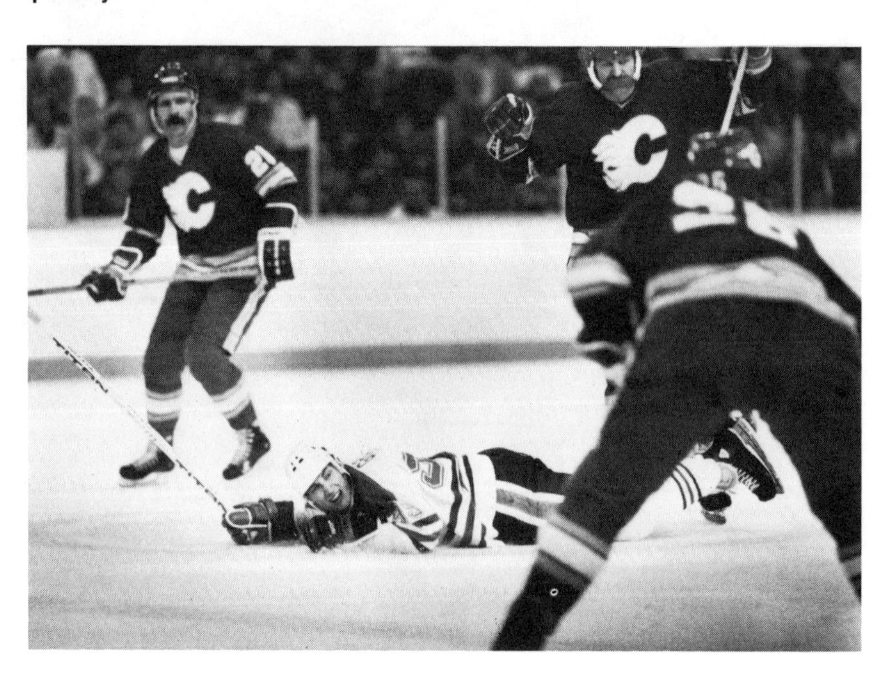

Not exactly the way to score 92 goals.

Game 76, vs. Flames at Calgary

The phone rang in the Gretzky home in Brantford. One of the kids was checking in.

"When Wayne telephoned, he said he'd get the 200th point in Calgary," Walter Gretzky explained. Walter and Phyllis Gretzky arrived in Calgary about three hours before the game. "I couldn't stay another game, so I guess we put a little pressure on Wayne to do it tonight. We have two sons in tournaments back home."

The Gretzkys were about the only people in the Corral who were rooting for Wayne to topple the Colossus of 200, a figure not even spoken about until this season. The Corral is only one of the NHL's 21 arenas in which Gretzky constantly is booed.

Gretzky and his Oilers have become the favorite sons of hated Edmonton and much of Canada, so they are showered with derision and insults by the Corral fans.

If anything, Gretzky is inspired by the taunting.

"He's too much of a professional to ever let that bother him," said Sather. "If anything, he gets psyched up by it."

Added Gretzky, with a twinkle in his eye, indicating immense self-satisfaction, "It's great the fans get behind their team. I don't care if they booed. They always do in Calgary."

The Oilers gave them plenty to boo as they stormed to victory 7-2 and Gretzky contributed two shorthanded goals on the same penalty, and two assists to vault the 200-point plateau.

Unlike Detroit and Buffalo, where he made everyone wait until the third period before denting the record books, Grezky owned this right from the beginning. After the teams went through a nine-minute span of feeling each other out, the Oilers got the first true scoring opportunity—thanks to guess who?

Gretzky lost a faceoff to Bridgman in the Calgary zone but he chased the puck to the side of the goal. Rookie defenseman Steve Konroyd had it but he was no match for Gretzky's magic. Wayne stole it and, in the same motion, fed Hughes near the top of the slot. Hughes' 20-foot slapshot whistled past Lemelin.

There was no wild celebrating, no special guest to present the puck to Gretzky. It was just another point, really, a typical Oiler scoring play in which Gretzky pressures an opponent into an error and, almost before anyone realizes he has done so, passes to a teammate for a goal. In many ways, it was anticlimactic, completely devoid of the drama of scoring No. 77, for instance.

Still, stop and think about what we're talking about. 200 points. Let it sink in. 200 points. 200.

Esposito was the first past 100, in 1968-69. It was no surprise that somebody exceeded 100 that season, though Espo was hardly the candidate—84 points was his previous high. Others—Stan Mikita, Bobby Hull, Bernie Geoffrion, Dickie Moore and, as far back as 1952-53, Howe had been in the upper 90s—indicated 100 points was coming. It was Espo who shattered it.

"There was a lot of talk about 100," recalled Esposito. "It wasn't a great leap to get there from what the top scorers had been getting."

Expansion from the original six to the current 21 teams has certainly helped the scorers of today. The competition isn't as stiff, the opposition isn't that familiar with your strengths and weaknesses and the goaltending can't be compared with 15 or 20 years ago.

Still, this assist was Gretzky's 200th point. No matter how much the game has been diluted, that is incredible, something even the greats of the past marvel at.

Richard, for instance, is a big Gretzky fan. Considering that the "Rocket," the first player to complete the 50-in-50 goals feat (in 1944-45; prior to that, no one had ever gotten as many as 40 goals in the 50-game seasons the NHL played), rarely hands out compliments, his words on Gretzky and 200 points carry added significance.

"Either he's very good or everyone else has become very bad," said Richard. "I'm certain it's that Gretzky is so much better than the rest. He has the greatest moves I've ever seen.

"The quality of the game is much worse than when I played. With all the emphasis on scoring the last few years, a team quits when it falls behind by two or three goals, and you get all those 10-2 and 12-4 games you see.

"But Gretzky doesn't get everything in games that are one-sided," added Richard, mentioning that Wayne usually is the reason Oiler games become runaways. "He's a born scorer and, if he had played in the 50s or 60s, he

The puck that brought Gretzky the 200th point.

would have been the best scorer in the NHL. He would have led the league whenever he played, though he would not have gotten so many points.

"He would not have gotten 200."

But now he had 200. Time to add to it.

It took only two more minutes for Gretzky to start on the third set of 100 points. With the Flames two men down, Gretzky worked the puck away from Calgary defenseman Bob Murdoch, then steered clear of forward Lanny McDonald near the corner. His pass to Semenko at the edge of the crease was, of course, perfect. Semenko stuffed it home for one of the easiest goals he'll ever score. And, though Gretzky had done all the work, he, too, had made it look easy.

The Flames moved within 2-1 before the period ended but they made the mistake of forgetting that Gretzky is an awesome offensive force, even while defending.

Goal No. 80 came on a Calgary power play when Gretzky's low slapshot from 40 feet handcuffed Lemelin. Just to show it was no fluke, Gretzky scored again 27 seconds later, this time on a wrist shot to the lower corner of the net that just snuck in by the right post.

"Those two shorthanded goals were the most important of the game," he said, for the moment ignoring the assist which gave him 200 points. "They turned the game our way.

"I was really excited to get the 200th point but it was the two shorthanded goals which meant the most to the team."

Ah, the team. Yes, folks, this scoring machine, this 21-year-old kid who could proclaim his greatness around the globe without dispute, was talking team.

"He's the ultimate team player," said Sather. "He's probably the most unselfish guy we have. Wayne's not playing for himself. He's playing for the team and he doesn't want to lose at anything."

Wayne's mother remembers his having the same fiery competitiveness when he was growing up. What she can't recall is spotting the skills which have made him the most dangerous scorer in hockey history.

"He was out on the rink in the backyard every day before school," she said. "Then he would skate again during noon hour, after school and again after supper. I had to make sure he did all his homework.

"He was so small. I knew how much he loved the game, that he loved everything about it. Not just the games but the practices, suiting up, even shoveling snow off the rink, I think. But I never really thought much about his being good enough to play in the NHL.

"Until he made the WHA, I never realized Wayne would play professional hockey. Once he made it in the WHA, I knew he was on his way."

Phyllis Gretzky seemed genuinely thrilled to have witnessed Wayne's scaling of the 200-point mountain, which he seems capable of turning into a mole hill with future scoring exploits. She had missed the game in Buffalo when he broke the goal mark because "Brent was in a tournament in Montreal," and so was she.

"We always went to Wayne's tournaments when he was only 10," she said. "Now we go to Brent's. Wayne understands and doesn't mind, he wants it this way. He wants us to treat all the kids the same."

"All the kids" include Wayne's sister Kim, 18; Keith, 15; Glenn, 12, and 10-year-old Brent. Keith is the one featured along with Wayne in a 7-Up commercial—Keith is the precocious one who, after watching along with his friends as Wayne showboats with the puck, claims, "I taught him everything he knows."

"All the publicity has put pressure on the other boys," noted Phyllis. "It's kind of rough for Keith but the others are young enough that it hasn't

All in the family. Brothers Keith, Glenn, and Brent.

bothered them yet.

"All the boys know how to handle themselves all right."

Now that Gretzky had made 200 points a topic of discussion, he wanted to discuss it. And not just in terms of Wayne Greetzky's achieving it.

"It is a lot of points," he admitted, "and, hopefully, I can go after it again. You have to stay healthy all year and not hit a lot of slumps or any long slumps. And you need to have a team that is a winner, with guys who score to take some of the pressure off you.

"A lot of pressure is off us now and we can concentrate on other goals we've established and team play.

"I think there are other players in the NHL who can come up to 200. Bossy, Trottier, (Dale) Hawerchuk of Winnipeg if he keeps improving, some others. Those guys are great scorers and on good teams, they might have a shot. You never can aim for 200, though, until you get close to it."

Nor can you stop a Wayne Gretzky from hitting it when he gets close to it, as the Flames learned.

"We're a tough team," said Flames coach Al MacNeil. The day before the game, MacNeil said his club would make it "very difficult" for Gretzky to move above the 199 mark he reached in Edmonton's game with Calgary five days earlier. "But we didn't have a lot of life. Our players didn't do what they should and Gretzky took advantage of it.

"You never see Gretzky slowing down. We coasted right into a loss. The shorthanded goals were brutal. You don't try to play the puck against Gretzky. He'll turn you inside-out."

He'll even turn the fans' sentiments inside-out. As the Oilers filed off the ice following the rout, the people inside the Corral rose and gave Grezky a standing ovation.

Game 77, vs. Rockies at Colorado

The next-to-last home game in the history of the Colorado Rockies. If the Oilers had come to Denver more often, and Gretzky had been able to draw more sellout crowds to the arena, then the Rockies wouldn't have needed to pull up stakes after the season and move to New Jersey.

This final meeting of the season between the Rockies and Oilers was not particularly relished by Edmonton.

"We had to leave Calgary at 6:30 in the morning," said Gretzky. "It took a lot out of us. We played one of our best games of the season against the Flames. But we were dog-tired for the Rockies."

Their weariness was most evident in the late stages of a sloppy, wide open contest in which Colorado rallied for a pair of goals to tie the Oilers 6-6. Edmonton had come back from a 4-2 deficit to grab a 6-4 lead, with Gretzky scoring once and setting up two other goals.

This was the kind of game the Oilers should have won. It was played at the rapid pace they like. Puckhandlers were given plenty of ice to roam and loads of clearance for shots at the goalies, Resch for Colorado, Low for Edmonton.

Yet, the Oilers managed only a tie. Too often, passes to teammates who had broken free were off-target. Dead-on shots were sailing wide or directly into the midsection of Resch. Forwards were drifting offside on 3-on-2 and even a 4-on-2 rush.

Gretzky got an assist on Kurri's tip-in in the first period. In the middle period, he feathered a pass from the right of the Colorado net to Messier in the slot and Messier powered a slapper past Resch with Edmonton on a power play, pulling the Oilers within 4-3.

That goal was the Oilers' 399th of the season, tying the NHL record set by the 1970-71 Boston Bruins, anchored, of course, by Esposito and Orr.

It seemed only natural that the Oilers would become the first team to score 400 goals in a season on a Gretzky tally. But, sometimes, doin' what comes naturally isn't the way things are done in sports.

Lumley got No. 400 with a stuff shot past Resch after he had retrieved a loose puck. Gretzky was not involved.

To make up for missing on that record, Gretzky put the Oilers ahead just a little later.

"That was one of the most freaky goals I scored all year," he said. "I took the puck at our blue line after it hit a Rockies' defenseman's stick in the corner and bounced right back to me."

Gretzky headed for enemy territory and took a slapshot from the top of the slot. It ticked off the stick of Colorado center Kevin Maxwell. That slight redirection fooled Resch and No. 99 had Goal No. 91.

Maxwell was the main checker used by Rockies coach Marshall Johnston when Gretzky was blanked in a 5-2 Oiler loss on March 6, snapping Wayne's consecutive-game points streak at 24. Oddly, this goal came on one of the few shifts that Maxwell played opposite him.

"They used a different shift against me tonight than the last time," said Gretzky, who was now up to 206 points. "I faced (defenseman) Rob Ramage more than Maxwell."

Wayne was disheartened that the Oilers had blown a point against such a poor team and just about eliminated themselves from finishing first in the overall standings. He wondered if people were looking too far ahead.

"It's not enough just to be in the playoffs," he said. "You've got to come up to them in the right frame of mind and playing the way you want to be all through the playoffs. We sure weren't at our best tonight."

Gretzky hinted that he still felt 100 goals were within reach, even with just three games left.

"Two are against Los Angeles and I've been real fortunate (to say the least; destructive would have been a better word) against the Kings," he said "If I'm going to bet, I'd use someone else's money, but the record (100 goals) is not out of the question."

According to Don Cherry, former coach of the Bruins and Rockies who was doing analysis on the broadcast of the game, nine goals in three games wouldn't be such a magnificent feat against the Rockies. Cherry saw all the wrong ways of trying to stop Gretzky when he watched the strategy employed by Colorado.

"They all worry about checking Gretzky," said Cherry, "and they forget there are other players. Heck, Messier's got 45 (goals). There's no way you can let a guy like that stand loose while the rest of the team scoots over to Gretzky.

"He'll see that and kill you. Before you get within a couple of feet, he'll make a move and get free or he'll pass it to the open man. Or he'll still shoot it in.

"When Maxwell takes Gretzky out of the play, big deal. The puck's in the net anyway because somebody else has scored. Then, they'll say he did a good job checking Gretzky. Phooey!"

Wayne Gretzky, 20 year old hockey superstar dining with Penthouse Pet Carol Davies.

Game 78, vs. Kings at Los Angeles

Los Angeles was going to get a bonus. The Kings had played such a major part in Gretzky's records that they had earned at least three extra shots at the Oilers. Edmonton, having run away with the Smythe Division, earned the right to meet the most inept of the division's playoff qualifiers. Hello, Kings.

So Gretzky would make at least one more trip to Southern California after this, the last regularly scheduled game at the Fabulous Forum between the teams. The best-of-five opening round in the chase for Lord Stanley's Cup would begin with a pair of tilts in Edmonton, then switch to LA for Game 3 and, if necessary, Game 4.

The Kings had to be grateful for small favors. After such a poor season, on the ice and at the gate, at least they could count on one sizable crowd in the playoffs. They may have stood no chance of beating the Oilers in the playoffs —as most pundits were surmising—but at least Gretzky and friends would fill the coffers for an extra night.

A crowd of 16,005—the 16th straight sellout the Oilers had attracted away from Edmonton—filled the Forum. If Los Angelinos appreciate anything, it's star quality, and there is no bigger star in sports than Gretzky.

Gretzky gave the fans a solid show with a goal and an assist in a 6-2 wipeout of the Kings. But he was a bystander as the Oilers set yet another league record.

Just 14 seconds into the game, Messier, who was staging a late drive for 50 goals, hit for No. 47. Ten seconds later, Lumley took a pass from Lowe and beat goalie Doug Keans to make it 2-0.

"Lightning strikes!" was Lumley's assessment. "I knew we were explosive, but two goals that quick has to surprise anyone."

Pittsburgh held the previous mark of two goals in 29 seconds on December 6, 1980.

"Something like that has to be demoralizing," said Gretzky. "There's a big crowd in the arena and the fans are ready to see their team do well and we go up 2-0 after 24 seconds."

And they did it with Gretzky not having reported to work yet.

"We're a team and all of our records are team records," he said. "Something like that shows we can all do the job."

By the end of the period, Edmonton led 4-0 and Gretzky had picked up his 116th assist, setting up Anderson's power-play goal. Anderson also got the Oilers' fourth goal.

Edmonton was able to coast the rest of the way. Messier was the most excited Oiler after stepping even closer to the coveted 50 with his 48th goal in the second period on a breakaway. Gretzky scored No. 92 just 1:50 into the final session.

Wayne's goal came thanks to a pass from Anderson, who was standing behind the Kings' net.

"I'm not sure if Wayne taught me that play," said Anderson. "But after watching him set up so many of us from back there, I was dying to try it."

Gretzky converted the pass from 10 feet up the slot, indoctrinating rookie goalie Mike Blake to life against the Oilers. Blake, who had been brought up from Saginaw of the International Hockey League a week earlier, now was in good company. If he never achieves another thing or plays another NHL game, he'll always be able to tell how he was victimized by The Great Gretzky.

Gretzky felt the game was important, even though the Oilers couldn't improve themselves in the standings in any way—the Islanders already had clinched the overall points title. Then again, Gretzky never feels any game, even an exhibition contest or a pickup game in the summer, is without significance.

"We were conscious of not having beaten them the last two times we played," he said. "We came in here against a sellout crowd and were up for the game and took it right to them.

"We know we're going to play them in the playoffs, so we want to have them off-balance and thinking about how we were able to beat them. Tonight's game will help.

"The Kings have been playing a disciplined game but we'll be ready for them in the playoffs. We had to let them know that tonight."

The Kings knew even before they were manhandled by Messier, Anderson, Lumley and, of course, Gretzky.

Dionne, the Kings' resident offensive genius and a man who, in 10 years, probably will be the answer to a hockey trivia question—Who was the last player to win the scoring crown before Gretzky?—offered this assessment of his adversary.

"He makes all of us look like bums," said the Kings' star. "I guess his next goal will be 300 points and there is not one guy in the league who will say he won't do it. He's just one of a kind. There's nobody close to him. I've seen Orr and Lafleur and Perreault at their best and there's no comparison.

"They say the league is more wide open but you don't see anybody else even close to Gretzky in points. Maybe he wouldn't have gotten 200 a few years ago but he still would have been way out there without anybody else challenging him."

Dionne has known for a couple of years that Gretzky is "something else," and that the word impossible was not in Wayne's vocabulary. But it wasn't until the Canada Cup that Dionne fully realized the extent of Gretzky's talents.

"All you have to do is give him the puck," explained Dionne, about whom the same thing used to be said but to a lesser degree because Marcel never demolished the scoring race like Gretzky did. "He has such great anticipation. I had thought Lafleur had the quickest hands I'd ever seen. Even Bossy, I thought he was up there. Gretzky is even better.

"Those other guys, you pretty much know what they are capable of doing. But Gretzky . . . he always has a new move, a new play, and it's always a great one."

Having played near Hollywood for seven years, Dionne is qualified to assess what makes a star, at least on the ice. He claims Gretzky possesses all the necessary ingredients.

"There are probably 10 things that make a star and Wayne has all of them," said Dionne. "Things like great anticipation, stamina, unbelievable moves that some of the best (NHL players) didn't have. People always are searching for bad things about his game. I hear them say he hasn't got a hard shot but how hard do you have to shoot it if you're as accurate as he is? If you always can hit the open spot the goalie can't cover, how hard do you have to shoot the puck?"

Mike Murphy, an 11-year veteran and a fine checker, is one of hockey's most astute players. In his prime, he was a consistent scorer as well as a standout defensive player. He has a deep knowledge of the game.

Murphy also feels Gretzky has no peer.

"He's just an amazing player," said Murphy. "You hear how the game has changed and everything is scoring and wide open, and that he wouldn't be doing what he is 10 or 15 years ago. I can't agree.

"Gretzky is an exceptional player, physically and mentally. He would have been one of the best regardless of the era. What's most amazing, even scary, is that he's 21. He's going to get better."

As Gretzky improves, Dionne might prosper.

"I told a friend of mine when we were in Buffalo early in the season that Gretzky'd get 200 points," Dionne recalled. "He had about 40 or so but I figured he could get five or six points a night. We made a friendly bet, $25."

Dionne didn't say whether he planned to cut Gretzky in on the wagering coup.

Game 79, vs. Kings at Edmonton

The 100-goal dream died as Gretzky managed only three assists against the Kings, who fell 7-3. The victory stretched Edmonton's late-season unbeaten string to eight, which seemed a positive harbinger for the playoffs.

Though Gretzky entered the game eight goals away from the century mark, few people—Wayne included—had given up hope of his reaching 100 in the last two games. He already had 13 goals against the beneficent Kings, including those two four-goal sprees. Another big game against LA would set him up for a final assault on 100.

On the surface, this seemed to be a meaningless game. Except for the possibility that Gretzky would break loose and move closer to the one galaxy he'd left unexplored, the Oilers had little interest in the game. The main objective was to stay healthy.

LA, however, had a good reason to try to beat the Oilers. Another lopsided loss would send the Oilers storming into the first round of the playoffs against the Kings, who could have little confidence in their chances, judging by the regular season.

The Kings opted to play it rough. While referee Bruce Hood was handing out 134 penalty minutes in the first period, LA opened up a 3-1 lead, with Jim Fox getting a pair of goals. Gretzky picked up an assist on Siltanen's power-play goal late in the period.

The teams clamped down in the second period, which was scoreless, but the rough stuff began again in the final stanza, when the Oilers scored five unanswered goals.

Messier got two goals and an assist and reached the 50-goal mark with 23 seconds left, on an assist by Gretzky. Wayne also set up Hunter's 16th goal.

"I wasn't really thinking about two goals tonight," said Messier. "But Wayne said, 'Go for it' after I got the first one.

"We went out in the third period and showed them they can't get anything out of this rink. I think that was important, to show them it's tough to win here."

Lumley found plenty of incentive in the game.

"We've played them four times in the last couple of weeks," he said. "You remember the little grudge; you remember the little things each player has done to you and when you only have three or four days to wait, you remember it all more."

Gretzky also found enough motivation, aside from the natural spur of setting records, and took a great deal of satisfaction from the win.

"To me, helping Mark get to 50 was as important as anything I could do for myself," he admitted. "I mean, I got my 50, and then I scored 60, 70, whatever. These guys are going for 50, 40, 30. That's not only important to them but to the whole team. They're going to be inspired when they go after these goals and that helps all of us, including me, play better."

Even though Gretzky expressed no disappointment at falling short of 100 goals—"I guess it wasn't meant to be but you have to leave yourself some things to go after"—some of his teammates and his coach were disappointed.

"When you're this close," said Sather, holding his hands a couple of inches apart, "you should have a chance to get it. You may never have the chance again."

"What's the difference between 96 and 100?" asked Fogolin. "Well, 96 is only four away and would have been great. Still, it's only four away. It would have been great to help him get it.

"It's still fantastic. It can't make him any better if he misses 100 by a couple of shots or ends up with 102. He's still all by himself in this game."

Game 80, vs. Jets at Edmonton

The most incredible offensive season in hockey history came to an end without fireworks. At the finish, Gretzky displayed little of the magic he weaved on NHL opponents throughout his unparalleled assault on the record books. There were no mad dashes for the 100-goal mark, no wild shootouts during which he smashed even more records.

In the 80th game, a lacklustre affair with the Winnipeg Jets, Edmonton was a 2-1 winner. Gretzky assisted on the decisive goal, the Oilers' second power-play tally within 72 seconds in the first period. Mainly, however, both teams were trying to avoid injury as they prepared for the playoffs.

"It's been tough to be interested in a lot of games, including this one, the last couple of weeks," Gretzky said. "We found it was only easy to get ready for teams we know we'll have a chance to meet in the divisional playoffs.

"Otherwise, after we had the division clinched and couldn't finish first overall, we didn't have much to aim for. We wanted to keep playing well for the playoffs and not let down. But we couldn't get the same intensity for these games."

Gretzky's final totals were 92 goals, 120 assists and 212 points. That's 16 more goals than anyone had ever compiled in a season, 11 more assists than his own mark and a whopping 48 points more than he got the previous year, when he broke Esposito's record of 152 points with 164.

In addition, there were the 10 hat tricks: the five-goal explosion against Philadelphia that brought him to 50 goals in 39 games; three four-goal games, two against Los Angeles and one against Quebec, and six three-goal contests.

"I'm very pleased with what I accomplished this year and with what the team did," said Gretzky. "This will always be a memorable season. The Oilers went from 14th in the NHL to second. We proved we belonged at the top of the league all year and that's something to be very proud of."

And what of the records?

"Of course, it's a cliche, but records are made to be broken," he noted. "If I stay healthy and the team keeps improving, I feel I should improve too. I think if that happens, I can challenge the numbers I got this year."

But this was a season of much more than numbers. Gretzky dominated his sport like nobody ever has. Not even Orr, who could turn the direction of a game around with one of his patented, rink-length rushes that so exhilirated everyone who saw it, ever posted the kind of statistics Gretzky turned in.

Gretzky did it under intense pressure from the media and, somewhat unintentionally, from the NHL. Hockey is a weak fourth among the major team sports in the States. Basically, it has a regional appeal—when the national television networks attempted to broadcast the sport in the 1960s and 70s, large sections of the U.S. opted for alternative programming. Hockey, the national game of Canada, a passion play on ice for people from the Maritimes to Victoria, played weakly in Peoria and not at all in the South, Southwest and West in the U.S.

In Gretzky, the NHL had a tremendously marketable commodity. Here was Wilt Chamberlain averaging 50 points a game or Lou Brock stealing 118 bases. And it was all rolled into a 21-year-old kid who looked like he never shaved (even though he is a spokesman for Bic razors) and was a model of decorum on and off the ice.

None of that goon stuff for Gretzky, one of the cleaner players in a game plagued by overpublicized brutality. He played by the rules and broke all the records.

So, while Gretzky was the latest hockey superstar to Canadians, the replacement for Lafleur who took over for Clarke who followed Esposito and Orr at the top—you can go all the way back to the NHL's first scoring sensation, Joe Malone in the late 1910s and through the 20s—he was the white knight on whose shifty shoulders the NHL could ride right back onto the American tube. And into prosperity, a land few of the 21 NHL teams have recently visited.

For now, the well-being of the National Hockey League is, in great part, in the hands of the skinny kid from Brantford. The league—and the sport—could do a lot worse.

The Playoffs

No need for suspense: the Oilers did not win the Stanley Cup. They didn't come close.

In the space of a week, the magic deserted them. The race for first place in the overall standings, the mammoth attention centered on the team and, of course, Gretzky's incomparable season had taken a great deal of steam out of the players.

Furthermore, they weren't properly prepared for the playoffs. While they were blitzing so many opponents, the Oilers weren't learning enough. They didn't suffer enough (just ask any New York Islander how important the pain of early failures has been in their ultimate success).

This was a group of babes in the hockey woods with a 19-year-old in goal and few time-tested veterans to rally around. As great as Gretzky is and will be, he cannot carry a team alone, and he wasn't ready to do so.

The Kings may have been playing possum in the final week of the season, when they were blown out twice by Edmonton. At any rate, LA coach Perry had drilled his team well on what to expect in the playoffs.

Game 1, at Edmonton

Neither the Oilers or Kings were known for defensive skills and they proved why in the opener of the best-of-five series. The teams combined for 18 goals, including seven in each of the first two periods.

When the Oilers grabbed a 4-1 lead 9:01 into the game, nearly everyone was expecting a rout. History—at least recent history, vintage 1981-82—told them so. But nobody told the Kings.

"Perry kept going up and down the bench, telling us to think about one goal at a time when we were down 4-1," offered Dave Taylor, the Kings' fine right wing who had a goal and three assists. "It was like a scrimmage. The last team to score wins."

After Gretzky had set up two goals by Siltanen, the second with Taylor penalized, to make it 4-1, Jim Fox and Taylor brought LA closer. Taylor's goal, with Gretzky off the ice for tripping, came with just seven seconds left in the period.

"That was the big goal," said Perry. "You get those late in a period and it psyches you for the next period. Plus, it makes them think about the big lead they're blowing."

The Kings outscored Edmonton 5-2 in the second period, when Fuhr looked shaky and the defense was worse. Gretzky managed an assist on a goal by Lumley but rookie Daryl Evans scored twice to offset that.

"We can't expect to get into a shootout with them and win," Dionne had said before the game. "But if we keep it close, anything can happen."

Anything was happening and the Oilers weren't sure they could cope. But when Gretzky beat Lessard in the LA goal at 10:20 and Hagman tied it two minutes later, all seemed right.

"I was sure we'd win after that," Lumley insisted.

They wouldn't. Only 2:36 after Hagman tied it, Taylor's shot ricocheted off the leg of Charlie Simmer and past Fuhr to make it 9-8.

"It hit the metal," said Simmer, who had a pin inserted in a broken right leg the previous season. "One of my more artistic goals."

The Oilers, realizing they never should have been in such a predicament —remember Messier's comment in the next-to-last game of the season that the Oilers had proved to LA that "they can't get anything out of this rink"— made an all-out assault for the tying marker. With 1:12 left, they got the opportunity they sought.

Gretzky took a pass from Kurri at the red line and sped around the defense. Lessard, who had NEVER stopped Gretzky on a breakaway ("not even in practice for the Canada Cup," he said), stopped the runaway express.

"He's tried that move on me before," said Lessard. "He fakes it and as I move, the puck keeps going right in by itself. He beat me all the time like that. But I got lucky this time."

Bernie Nicholls, another Kings' rookie, applied the finishing touch with an empty-net goal and the Kings had stolen Game 1—and the home-ice edge.

They'd done it by converting four times on the power play after a streak of just two power-play goals in the last 30 chances. They'd beaten the highest scoring team in NHL history at its own game.

The next day, when a newspaper headline proclaimed, "OH MY GAWD," then the story proceeded to dissect what went wrong, one could see that the Oilers were in for a most strenuous test.

Game 2, at Edmonton

The Oilers indicated early that they meant business when Hughes beat Lessard on a breakaway with the game less than two minutes old. They kept the Kings away from Fuhr for most of the first period, with six of LA's seven shots harmless.

Lessard kept it at 1-0 when he made a miraculous save on Gretzky in the opening period. With Edmonton shorthanded, Gretzky had an open net, only to see Lessard dive back across the crease to stop the shot.

The Kings' rookies went to work in the second period. Nicholls scored behind a pick by Taylor with a 40-foot slap-shot; then Evens took advantage of Messier's misplay. Messier lost the puck in front of the Edmonton net and Evans poked it into the corner with Fuhr helpless and shocked at his teammate's transgression.

The Kings had shifted the flow in their favor once more, outshooting Edmonton 18-5 over the last 15 minutes of the period. And Lessard was stopping everything sent his way.

"We were getting a little frustrated," said Gretzky. "We kept going at him and going at him and getting nothing."

With less than five minutes remaining in regulation, Kurri got something. He took a drop pass from Huddy and slammed a rising slapshot over Lessard's shoulder to tie it.

"We began to breathe a little easier then," said Gretzky. "We felt confident we'd win it in OT."

Fittingly . . . naturally . . . inevitably, Gretzky was the one who won it.

"I just remembered what we said before the overtime, that everybody should shoot at the net," he said.

Gretzky got his chance a little over six minutes into the extra session. The Kings were tentative and it was out of their timidity that Gretzky pounced.

Lessard had swept Huddy's shot into the left wing corner, where Kings defenseman Larry Murphy tried to clear it. But the puck bounced right to Gretzky as LA's Doug Smith and Fox collided. Gretzky's shot from the top of the left faceoff circle behind a Lumley screen zipped by Lessard.

"We both turned and ran into each other," said Fox. "That gave him a second to set up and shoot. I would've been happier if it'd been somebody else."

"The puck bounced between us," noted Smith. "I reached for his stick but it was a split second too late. I turned around and the puck was in the net."

"Basically, I was just shooting it," Gretzky admitted. "Unless you are shooting point-black, I think nine of 10 times you just try to aim for the net."

Perry, who had done a masterful job of preparing his troops, was disheartened by the Kings' overtime play.

"I wanted to go at them the same way we did in the first three periods," he said, "but sometimes we have the tendency to sit back."

Sather expressed admiration for the Kings' efforts.

"I don't want anyone to think we've been panicking," he warned. "The Kings are a good team and they're not going to fold up for anyone."

Game 3, at Los Angeles

Wild!

LA's success in Edmonton brought out an SRO crowd of 16,005, the third sellout of the season for the Kings, all against the Oilers. For those fans who stuck with the team, the rewards this night would be plentiful.

Playing like the Oilers everyone expected to see, Edmonton built a 5-0 lead after two periods. As the Oilers controlled play, the fans became venemous towards Edmonton and the worst taunts were hurled at Gretzky.

He had scored twice and contributed two assists as the Oilers zoomed into the apparently safe lead. Gretzky's first tally was while killing a penalty. After Fuhr had stopped Dionne cold, Gretzky captured the puck and skated across the Kings' blue line. He buried defenseman Jerry Korab into the ice with a typical move, cut to his left as Evans tried to stick him, then brushed off Simmer's stick check to skate into the left wing circle. His low shot scooted past Lessard, who had come well out of the net.

While most fans would have "oohed and aahed" at his majestic display, the Forum fans booed Gretzky and Kings GM George Maguire slammed the table in front of him with his fist.

That wondrous goal came with 37 seconds left in the first period. Only 43 seconds into the next session, while killing the same penalty, Edmonton struck again.

Gretzky passed to Fogolin, then cut towards the net, with two checkers following him. Fogolin had plenty of room and, after faking Korab, put a slap-shot past Lessard for 3-0.

Siltanen took a pass from Gretzky and ripped a shot which went right through the net for a 4-0 Oiler advantage, then Gretzky tipped in a pass from Anderson on a power play and it was 5-0.

By this point, the game had gotten chippy. It was to worsen in the dramatic third period which, to the Oilers, must have seemed to have been penned by Rod Serling for a "Twilight Zone" episode.

That Twilight Zone look.

"The place: the Fabulous Forum in Inglewood, California. The time: spring, 1982. A bunch of young men on skates have been mauling another group. These young men, known as the Edmonton Oilers, seem like the National Hockey League's version of destiny's children. What they don't realize is that, for the next 22 minutes and 35 seconds, they will be travelling through time and space to a place known as the 'Twilight Zone.' "

Jay Wells began LA's resurgence with his second goal of the season on a screen shot at 2:36. Before Smith put a rebound of a Mark Hardy shot just under the crossbar at 5:58, Kings owner Jerry Buss had left the arena.

The Oilers steadied themselves and held their 5-2 lead through a brawl and the next 8½ minutes. Then Simmer, standing in one of Gretzky's favorite spots—behind the enemy net—tried to pass the puck in front and it deflected off Oilers defenseman Randy Gregg and past Fuhr.

The goal pumped new life into the Kings and they immediately began to exploit a tired Edmonton defensive corps. With 4:01 to go, and the crowd boisterously supporting the Kings—and just as boisterously exercising their perogative and hurling epithets at the Oilers—Hardy took a drop pass from Steve Bozek, went around Fuhr—who made a bad move by leaving his net too soon—and, with Gretzky trying to guard the net, put the puck past Wayne's stick on a power play.

The Oilers were reeling but they still held a one-goal margin. It looked like enough as Lessard was lifted for another attacker but the Kings weren't getting anywhere.

Then, suddenly, as suddenly as the game began slipping away from the Oilers, it was tied. Bozek, yet another LA rookie (and their best freshman) backhanded the rebound of Hardy's shot from the top of the slot. It snuck through a maze of arms, legs and sticks and pads. With :05 showing on the clock, the puck settled into the net. It was 5-5.

The Oilers stayed under whatever spell the Kings had weaved just long enough for Evans to score his fourth goal in three playoff games. Smith beat Messier on a faceoff and sent the puck to Evans for a 25-foot slapshot that sailed over the right shoulder of Fuhr.

As the Kings rushed off the bench to congratulate Evans, you could almost hear that eerie music in the background. And Serling's voice, as cool and deceptive as always, saying something about the quirks of life in the "Twilight Zone."

The spoils of war: Gretzky on the set of MASH.

Game 4, at Los Angeles

Leading up to what could be the last game of the season for the Oilers, who were in shock over that possibility so early in the playoffs, came a war of words. Nasty words.

Wells accused Gretzky of being selfish and unwilling to put the team ahead of his personal gains.

"Wayne wasn't a team man, he was looking out for himself," said Wells about the third game. "That's what I said to him in the third period. He's just a player who likes to score goals. I consider him one of the worst team men in the league.

"He's got a team behind him that, when someone bumps him, the whole team is protecting him. But, if somebody else gets into it, Wayne's skating around center ice."

"Jay Wells is a nobody and never will be anybody," Gretzky retorted. "He's just trying to make a name for himself. I go out and do my job on the ice. Hopefully, he'll do his job, whatever that is."

Sather was upset with the Forum fans, mainly because the things they shouted at Gretzky rarely had anything to do with hockey, more often pertaining to his genealogy and sexual preferences.

"The people here have the least amount of class in North America," Sather said. "There were guys yelling obscenities even before the game started and they kept it up all night long. How would you like to have your family sitting at a game and hearing all that?

"They show a total lack of sophistication. California is supposed to be a very sophisticated place, but when the crowd starts saying a guy sucks . . . why would you take your kid and expose him to something like that?

"This was the worst display of courtesy I've seen in the 20 years I've been in hockey."

And the final 22:35 were the weirdest minutes he'd spent.

After all the verbal shenanigans, the Kings and Oilers got down to playing the best game of the series. The Oilers, facing an elimination of utmost embarrassment, won 3-2 as they held the Kings to 25 shots and made the most of the 21 they got at Lessard.

Kurri, Anderson and Hughes provided the goals and the Edmonton defense, so maligned thus far, threw a protective net around Fuhr when things got tight. It was an impressive performance under the most stressful conditions.

"We responded tonight. Now, we're going home to wrap this up," boasted Lumley. "We've made it hard on ourselves but now we're ready to end it."

Game 5, at Edmonton

The Kings had contributed mightily to the rise of the Oilers and especially to Gretzky's heavenly numbers. Edmonton went 5-1-2 against LA, including the 10-3 and 11-4 laughers in which Gretzky got four goals apiece. In all, the 13 goals and 22 points he scored against the Kings were the most he managed against anybody. The Oilers had outscored the Kings 51-27.

Surely now that the Oilers had tied the series, they would blast away the Kings in the decisive fifth game. Edmonton fans already were making airplane reservations for the next series, just 1½ hours away in Vancouver.

But the Kings, as Sather predicted, would not fold. They'd become a confident, even cocky bunch.

"After we came here and played so well in the first game, I knew the emotion and desire was there," said Perry. "That's when I knew we had a shot at it. But I downplayed it on purpose."

There was no downplaying the Kings' verve and mastery in the fifth game. From the beginning, they were the better team. Lessard made 39 saves and Fuhr could stop only 24 of 31 shots. The Kings won 7-4, with Simmer scoring twice and those two annoying rookies, Evans and Nichols, both fresh from the AHL, each scoring once.

Gretzky's sensational season ended in utter dismay. For all his achievements—he scored once in Game 5, giving him 97 goals for the year, including the playoffs—Wayne was crushed by the early exit from the chase for the Stanley Cup.

"I don't think I've ever been as disappointed," he said. "We were building towards the Cup and didn't even get past the first round. Hopefully, it's something we're going to learn from. We're so young that I don't know how we'll take it. It's up to the older guys"—he included himself, at 21, in that group—"to say let's not get down because of it. Let's do what it takes to go all the way the next time."

While they were being called everything from "chokers" to "wimps" in the local press, the Oilers realized a change in approach might be necessary. There was too much emphasis on the regular season and, quite possibly, on Gretzky's records. After six months, 80 games, there was nothing left.

The Kings wouldn't get beyond the next round. But their victory against heavy odds made their season.

"Because the Kings haven't done much in the playoffs for a long time," said Perry, "at least for five years, that is, they have scaled the first hurdle. I think they have the monkey off their backs."

The Oilers must carry that monkey into the 1983 playoffs. No matter how much they achieve during the regular season, it is a year which will be measured solely by their post-season performance.

Conclusion

When all the numbers were totaled, when all the accolades were handed out, two questions remained: why and what's next?

Why was Wayne Gretzky able to forge into the unknown, the unpredicted, the nearly incomprehensible? At a time when the 200-point mark was out in the distance somewhere, for somebody to challenge in the year 2,000, perhaps, why had Gretzky been able to move the clock up so far?

Many factors went into Gretzky's incredible season, his exquisite talent and flair not the least of them. But it was much more than the fact he is a superbly conditioned, coordinated and dedicated athlete.

Certainly the exhuberance of youth the Oilers carried through the season helped Gretzky. This was a group of teenagers and guys just out of their teens, spiced some by "old men" of 24 or so, who simply did not know any better. Why shouldn't they adopt an all-out assault style? Young legs and innocent minds.

The coaching staff aided him as well. There was no pampering of the superstar, which suited Gretzky just fine. Sather may have used him up in the regular season, but what else could the coach do?

"The best strategy as coach of this team," Sather said, "is to send No. 99 over the boards."

For the most part, that strategy worked, so why back away from it?

The era in which Gretzky plays is important too. As he said so many times during the season, hockey had once more become a wide open, gambling game. No style fits Gretzky better.

Perhaps the most significant ingredient was Gretzky's attitude. Not only is he blessed with skills and intelligence on the ice that border on the unfathomable, but he doesn't get flustered. He's always in control, whether running a power play, killing a penalty, inspiring his teammates or dealing with the fans, press and fellow players away from the rink.

As Esposito mentioned, "Wayne is a nice kid. He's always got time for everyone and he's always patient and cooperative."

Few people understand their importance, yet refuse to flaunt it, like Gretzky. And he's only 21.

Rodger Gottlieb, the NHL's director of media relations, spent a great deal of time with Gretzky during Wayne's drive to pass Esposito's goals mark. It was a chase which captured the imagination and interest of all sports fans, not just hockey addicts.

"As extraordinary as Wayne is on the ice, he's the same off the ice," said Gottlieb. "It amazed me the way he handled the pressure and media onslaught during his chase of Esposito's record. He was courteous and patient all the time, no matter who he was dealing with. He handled it better than any of us did.

"You have to remember that there were endless press conferences, after games and practices. There were television interviews locally and for the networks. And radio interviews. But he always had time for the fans, at the practice rinks, hotels, arenas.

"After he scored the three goals in Buffalo, Wayne went to a private party. Burt Reynolds and Goldie Hawn, who were shooting a film in Buffalo, were there. I'm sure it was a late night.

"Wayne had promised to be on 'Good Morning America' regardless of how much he celebrated. I called him at 6:40 in the morning and I half expected a tough retort. He just said, 'OK,' then met me down in the lobby a half-hour later. He could hardly keep his eyes open, but he did a terrific interview.

"Then he was asked if he minded sticking around for 'AM Buffalo,' to tape a few minutes, which he said he'd do. Then, on the way out, one of the local news guys asks for a minute spot and Wayne says fine."

Gottlieb recalled the early Gretzky, the kid who came out of the WHA with plenty of fanfare . . . and many doubters.

"When he first came into the league in 1979, his answers were almost stereotyped," said Gottlieb. "Now he puts thought and perspective into his answers. He's come a long way."

The best indication of Gretzky's ability to command respect without having people cower to him is the way he fits in with the Oilers. He is one of the boys. He takes part in clubhouse pranks, enjoys socializing with his teammates and doesn't allow anything that happens on the ice to infringe on his friendships with them.

"It really struck me in Detroit, when he got the 76th goal, that we were a part of history," added Gottlieb. "His teammates certainly felt that way. They

Walter Gretzky, Wayne's father.

were all scurrying around for programs before the game and I'd never seen that by pros.

"If Wayne was an egomaniac, he'd just say, 'Screw You,' to all of it. But I can't picture him ever doing that. I don't think anyone who knows him could imagine him being any different than he is."

Ziegler thinks Gretzky is the finest possible spokesman for the game, something the league could take more advantage of.

"I'm as proud of him off the ice as on the ice," said Ziegler. "When he was over in Finland, playing for Team Canada in the World Championships, they held a press conference for him. Historically, that was a first: a press conference for one man. It had never been done in the World Championships before.

"The first thing he was asked was, 'Wasn't it nice to play games in Europe, where there's no violence?' Wayne's answer was that he was subjected to more violence in the game the day before against Czechoslovakia than in the whole NHL season.

" 'And I have the welts and bruises to show you to prove it,' he said.

"Then he admitted it was a thrill to play for his country, that it was fine but he has three goals in hockey:

" 'No. 1 is to win the Stanley Cup. No. 2 is to win the Stanley Cup. No. 3 is to win the Stanley Cup.'

"If I sat for a month and tried to write a script for Wayne Gretzky, I never would have thought of something like that. Anything I could have written would never have been as effective as what he came up with on the spot.

"I would like to clone him as a human. He's been first class, cooperative, and he always tries to help the sport he's in," continued Ziegler. "What more can you ask from someone?"

Lots more will be asked from Gretzky. Even he admits that his peak seasons probably are several years off. Now that the 200-point barrier is a shattered memory, the public is going to expect further journeys into the near-impossible.

100 goals? 250 points? 300?

"The other guys on the team just watch him and shake their heads," said Sather. "They're in awe of him, just as I am. He knows what's going on all the time."

He knows. It's as if every game, every shift, every play, has taken place before for Wayne Gretzky. He is like a man out of the future, someone who knows all that has happened in the past and now is living through those occurrences. And determining how they happen.

THE GREAT GRETZKY

WAYNE GRETZKY'S PROFESSIONAL CAREER STATISTICS

Born, Brantford, Ontario, Canada, Jan. 26, 1961
Center. Shoots left. 5'11" 165 pounds
Last amateur club: Sault Ste. Marie Greyhounds (Jrs.)

REGULAR SEASON	CLUB	GP	G	A	PTS	PIM
1978-79	Indianapolis	8	3	3	6	0
	Edmonton	72	43	61	104	19
1979-80	Edmonton	79	51	86	137	21
1980-81	Edmonton	80	55	109	164	28
1981-82	Edmonton	80	92	120	212	26
	NHL TOTALS	239	198	315	513	75
	WHA TOTALS	80	46	64	110	19

PLAYOFFS	CLUB	GP	G	A	PTS	PIM
1978-79	Edmonton	13	10	10	20	2
1979-80	Edmonton	3	2	1	3	0
1980-81	Edmonton	9	7	14	21	4
1981-82	Edmonton	5	5	7	12	8
	NHL TOTALS	17	14	22	36	12
	WHA TOTALS	13	10	10	20	2

RECORDS SET BY WAYNE GRETZKY IN 1981-82

Most goals, one season	92
Most assists, one season	120
Most points, one season	212
Most games scoring three or more goals	10
Highest assists-per-game average	1.50
Highest points-per-game average	2.65
Fastest 50 goals at start of season	39 games
Largest margin as scoring leader	65 points

WAYNE GRETZKY'S SCORING STATISTICS, 1981-82

80 games
92 goals
120 assists
212 points
26 penalty minutes

18 power-play goals
6 shorthanded goals
12 game-winning goals
4 game-tying goals

HOW WAYNE GRETZKY FARED AGAINST EACH NHL TEAM

OPPONENT	GOALS	ASSISTS	POINTS
Boston	1	4	5
Buffalo	4	2	6
Calgary	9	11	20
Chicago	4	7	11
Colorado	5	11	16
Detroit	2	7	9
Hartford	5	3	8
Los Angeles	13	9	22
Minnesota	5	7	12
Montreal	1	6	7
NY Islanders	2	7	9
NY Rangers	4	5	9
Philadelphia	9	3	12
Pittsburgh	5	4	9
Quebec	4	5	9
St. Louis	6	4	10
Toronto	3	2	5
Vancouver	4	14	18
Washington	4	5	9
Winnipeg	2	4	6
TOTALS	92	120	212

About the Author

Barry Wilner is the hockey editor for The Associated Press and has been writing about the sport for eight years. He also has written a book about Soviet sports training techniques.